BEST OF JAPAN
YOUR #1 ITINERARY PLANNER FOR WHAT TO SEE, DO, AND EAT

Wanderlust Pocket Guides

Planning a trip to Japan?
Check other Wanderlust Pocket Travel Guides:

BEST OF TOKYO: YOUR #1 ITINERARY PLANNER FOR WHAT TO SEE, DO, AND EAT

BEST OF KYOTO: YOUR #1 ITINERARY PLANNER FOR WHAT TO SEE, DO, AND EAT

BEST OF TOKYO AND KYOTO BOOK SET

Table of Contents

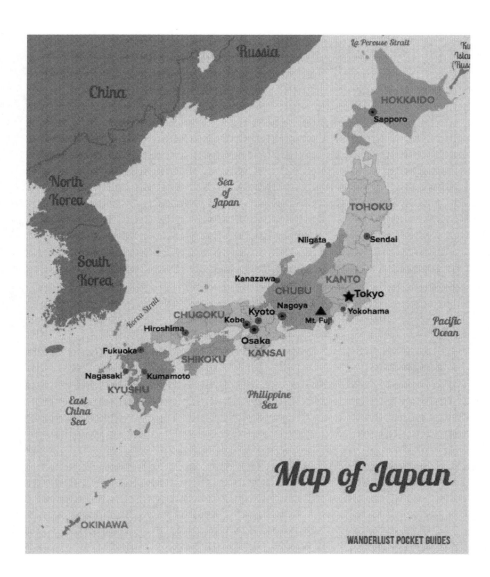

Map of Japan

WANDERLUST POCKET GUIDES

INTRODUCTION

Chances are, you've seen Japan on TV or in the movies, and it is always portrayed as a strange, strange place. From *Lost in Translation* to *Babel*, Japan seems to lend itself naturally as a puzzling environment for the western protagonist's life-changing experience. But what a unique, delicious, and entirely contradictory puzzle it is! Emerging from thousands of years of history and a deeply egocentric native culture, through heavy western influences, decades of aggressive imperial expansion, and the world's first nuclear attack, Japan has managed to transform and modernize itself with what seems like lightning speed.

A visit to Japan will inevitably take you through this long and complicated history. Where else in the world can you partake in hanami, the traditional custom of viewing cherry blossoms and other flowers in the spring that started in the 700's, in a Buddhist temple just as old, before heading to a robot burlesque show over dinner? The glittery co-exists with the rustic, the ultra-modern with the ultra-ancient. Luckily, with our guide, you don't have to choose - you can see all facets of this nearly mythical country, with an itinerary that you have customized and planned for yourself!

HOW TO USE THIS GUIDE

This guide consists of two major parts. In Part I, we talk about the core cities of Japan that you should go to if you only have a week or two - these cities are **Tokyo** and **Kyoto**, and of slightly lesser importance, **Hiroshima** and **Osaka**. Visiting these four cities is often considered the "**Golden Route**" of Japan. For each of these cities, we have provided tons of must-see sights you've dreamed of visiting, the most unique experiences you'll want to talk about for years, and the food that will tickle your taste buds like nothing before. There are also ample of recommendations for where to stay.

If you have a bit more time in Japan, navigate to Part II of this guide, where we discuss other destinations according to your interest. How about some **snorkeling** and **manta ray spotting** off of the coast of **Hokkaido**? Or take in the shimmery white castle in historical **Himeji**? You can even visit **an island full of just bunnies** or **cats**! There are plenty of places to visit for everyone - whether you are a history and culture lover, an outdoorsy type, or more interested in something off the beaten path.

Of course, feel free to mix and match when building your itinerary. This is your trip, after all, and we want to make sure you get your fill of Japan, no matter what you enjoy doing most!

SYMBOLS LEGEND

Sights and Attractions
(**) We indicate the absolutely must-see sights and attractions with two asterisks after their name.
(*) We indicate the highly recommended sights and attractions with one asterisk after their name.

Restaurants
Average meal cost:
$ - less than $10 (USD)
$$ - $11 USD - $ 25 (USD)
$$$ - $ 25 – 50 USD and up (USD)
$$$$ - $ 50 and up (USD)

Hotels
$ - less than $100 (USD)
$$ - $101- $150 (USD)
$$$ - $ 151 and up (USD)

PART I – THE GOLDEN ROUTE

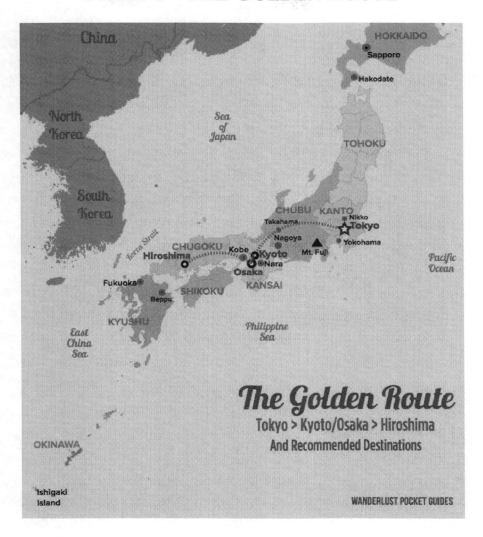

TOKYO

No other city typifies Japan, both old and new, as Tokyo does. Here in the capital, blinding neon lights are only a stone's throw away from the traditional sumo wrestling quarter, and you can find a steakhouse or an Irish pub just as easily as a traditional Japanese meal overlooking a tranquil garden. Even a cursory visit to this large metropolis will take at least a few days. We recommend budgeting 3 to 5 days before heading down to Kyoto.

Shinjuku District, Tokyo

What to See

Shibuya District

Shibuya is one of the busiest shopping and eating districts in Tokyo, popular especially with students and young office workers. It is considered less "crazy" than Shinjuku District, more down-to-earth than Harajuku District, and less international than Roppongi District, and offers a flavor of nightlife you won't find anywhere else. There are also more than a dozen department stores selling everything to designer clothes to plain houseware.

Shibuya Pedestrian Scramble is at the center of the district, and of Japan's avant-garde, ultra cool, bordering on strange at times youth and fashion culture. For the trendiest fashion, head to the Shibuya 109 shopping center.

Look for the intersection in front of the Hachiko exit of the Shibuya train station, with its overwhelming neon advertisements and giant video screens, which has become a popular filming spot for western filmmakers and one of the most recognizable spots in Japan.

Address: Exit from the Hachiko Exit at Shibuya JR Train Station.

Meiji Jingu (Meiji Shrine)
Stepping from the ultramodern, bustling streets of the Shibuya district into Meiji Jingu, you may feel as if you are traveling back in time to the 1800's, when this famous Shinto shrine was built and dedicated to the Emperor Meiji and his wife Empress Shoken. Located in an evergreen forest that covers 170 acres of prime real estate in Tokyo, this historical site consists of two precincts – the inner precinct, centered on the shrine building, which contains a museum that displays history and artifacts from the Meiji era; and an outer precinct, which includes the famous Meiji Memorial Picture Gallery, Meiji Memorial Hall, and the National Stadium.

Tips
Take a walk in nature, and experience a few hours of peaceful reprieve away from Shibuya's blinding neon lights in this sanctuary, while learning about an important period in Japanese history.
If you are lucky, you may run into Japan's dignitaries paying their respects in the central sanctuary.
Address: 1-1 Yoyogi Kamizonocho, Shibuya

Yoyogi Park
Yoyogi Park in the Harajuku district is the site of the first successful powered aircraft flight in Japan, in 1910. During the post-war American occupation, U.S. officers lived in the area, and in 1964, it was elected as the site for the 1964 Tokyo Olympics. The distinctive Olympic buildings designed by Kenzo Tange can still be seen nearby.

Today, with its beautiful pond and fountains, basketball court, soccer field and sports stadium, the park is a popular public hangout where people gather to hang out, play music, and practice martial arts.

Tips
You can rent a bike on site, and take a spin through the bike path.
Address: 2-1 Yoyogi Kamizonocho, Shibuya

Sensoji Temple
Built in the year 628 and dedicated to Kannon, the Buddhist goddess of mercy, Sensoji is one of the oldest temples in Tokyo. The original building was bombed and destroyed during World War II, but the rebuilt temple has since served as a symbol of peace and rebirth to the Japanese people. Each spring, the temple is also the focus of Tokyo's largest and most popular festivals, Sanja Matsuri, which features prominent parades, traditional music and dancing. Be sure to stop by the contemplative garden in the courtyard, and consult the oracle and divine answers to your most secret questions.

Tips
If you have time, also visit the Asakusa Shrine, a Shinto shrine, next door.
Nakamise-dōri, the street leading to the gate of the Sensoji Temple, features 89 shops selling souvenirs.

In the courtyard of the temple there is a tree that was hit by a bomb in the air raids, and it had regrown in the husk of the old tree and is a similar symbol to the temple itself.

Address: 2-3-1 Asakusa, Taito

Sakura (Cherry Blossoms)

Chidorigafuchi Park
If you are in town between April and early May, a visit to Chidorigafuchi to see Japan's famous cherry blossoms - sakuras - is a must. During the season, the park features acres of serene greenery right in the center of Tokyo, lines of sakura trees lining the river, and boat rides. You will often find professional photographers congregating in the park.

Tips
During sakura season, get to Chidorigafuchi before 10am to avoid crowds.
For the best view, enter through Kudanshita station and walk along the moat. You will be greeted by a great view of the Tokyo Tower behind sakura trees.
You can also rent a rowboat along the moat.

Address: 1-1 Kitanomarukoen, Chiyoda

Tokyo Skytree

Tokyo SkyTree, at 634 meters, is the second tallest structure in the world after the Burj Khalifa and the place to take in a panoramic view of Tokyo. The tower, located in the Sumida district, combines neofuturistic design with traditional Japanese aesthetics, and features observatories at 350 meters and 450 meters. For those not faint of heart, a section of glass flooring gives offers a direct downward view of the streets hundreds of meters below.There are also many restaurants, and a shopping mall in the same building.

Tips
On a clear day, you can see the entirety of Tokyo, as well as Mt. Fuji.
If you are not a Japanese citizen and bring your passport with you, you can skip the long ticket line and get your ticket at the foreigners' booth for a few extra bucks.
Lines are always long here. For alternative views of the city, check out Tokyo Metropolitan Government Office, or Tokyo Tower.

Address: 1-1-2 Oshiage, Sumida

View of Odaiba Island

Odaiba Island
Initially built for defense purposes in the 1850s, this man-made island located in the Tokyo Bay has since become way more fun with multiple shopping malls, restaurants, theme parks and futuristic architecture. Ride the Ferris wheel in Palette Town at night, visit Megaweb, an exhibition hall for Japanese carmaker Toyota, and get lost in Miraikan, the Museum of Emerging Science and Innovation where you can rub elbows with Asimo, Honda's very cute robot, you will want to spend at least a whole day in this fantastic town of the future.

Tokyo Tower
If the SkyTree is too crowded, try the views of this Eiffel Tower-inspired lattice tower that, at 1,092 feet, is the second tallest structure in Japan. The communications and observation tower located in the Shiba-koen district of Minato boasts of a view as stunning as that of the SkyTree, with two observatories, one at 490 feet, and one at 819 feet, as well as "FootTown", a four-story building directly under the tower which houses museums,

restaurants and shops. Like the Empire State Building, the Tokyo Tower changes its lighting arrangements for special events and holidays.

Address: 4 Chome-2-8 Shibakoen, Minato

Sanrio Puroland
Welcome Hello Kitty Wonderland! This indoor theme park, located in Tama New Town, is entirely devoted to the beloved cast of Sanrio cartoon characters - Hello Kitty and friends, My Melody, Cinnamoroll, Jewelpet, and many more. Theme rides include a boat ride in which Cinnamorroll leads parkgoers to a party being held by Hello Kitty, passing through the homes of several Sanrio characters, including Kerroppi's pond and Badtz Maru's cave. Visitors can also tour Hello Kitty's house with its Renaissance style family portraits, fancy furniture and a bathtub shaped like Kitty's face. Afterwards, check out the gift shop for Sanrio merchandise only available here!

Address: 1-31 Ochiai, Tama, Tokyo Prefecture

Tokyo Disney Resort
Come to Tokyo's Disney Resort, located in Urayasu, Chiba, for an experience at once familiar and unique to the western tourist. It is the 3rd most visited Disneyland in the world, and the 2nd to open outside the United States. Aside from "**Tokyo Disneyland**", a Magic Kingdom park just like the others, there is a sister park called "**Tokyo DisneySea**", a park theme based on nautical exploration, adventure, and different lands. There is also a shopping and entertainment complex called **Ikspiari**. Unlike its gargantuan Disney Resort counterpart in Florida, Tokyo's version is much smaller and can be thoroughly explored in roughly two days.

Address: 1-1 Maihama, Urayasu, Chiba Prefecture

Experiences

Fish Auction at Tsukiji Fish Market
Kabuki Theater
Sumo Wrestling Match
Special-themed Cafes
Hot spring bath at Oedo-Onsen-Monogatari
Shop for electronics at gamer and otaku-heaven Akihabara Districts
Shop at the Ginza District
Karaoke! The original, Japanese-style

Tsukiji Fish Market
An early morning filled with butchered fish heads, fish parts and raw fish, ought not to be appealing, yet Tsukiji Market has become an undeniably essential Tokyo experience. The largest fish market in Japan with 1,600 stalls selling more than 700,000 tons of fish each year, Tsukiji, located in the Chuo district, is the first stop for Tokyo's top sushi chefs each day, and as well as a haven for sushi lovers - it doesn't get fresher than this, unless you plan to do some diving before breakfast.

Come early if you want to see the famous tuna auction, which is limited to a maximum of 120 visitors. Tickets are issued on a first come, first serve basis beginning at 4:30am at the market's Fish Information Center, and the actual auction takes place between 5am and 6:15am. You will want to take a taxi, as the subway does not begin operating until 6am.
The market is divided into an inner, wholesale market, which is off-limits to visitors until after 9am, and an outer market, where you will find tons of interesting shops. One shop specializes in dried seaweed, while another sells only bowls of every shape and size imaginable. Take a walk after your sushi breakfast, and pick up something unique.

Tips

Avoid the tourist trap food stalls on the way to the market, and go for the real deal at the market itself.

Don't wear clothes you are attached to - water (at times bloody) can splash while fish containers are being moved.

The workers don't mind visitors or being photographed (no flash), as long as you don't get in the way of their business

Show up early! Aside from the auction, activities at the market slow after 8am in the market, and many shops will close by 10am.

Address: 5 Chome-2-1 Tsukiji, Chuo

Kabuki-za Theater
There is no better place to experience Kabuki, the beautiful and mysterious classical Japanese dance-drama, than at the Kabukiza. Japan's most famous and most grand Kabuki theater, Kabukiza dates back to 1889, though the original structure has been destroyed and rebuilt 4 times in its lengthy history. More than other theaters around Japan, Kabuki-za is famous for the stylization of its programs, and the elaborate makeup worn by its performers.

Tips
The best way to experience Kabuki is to attend a single act, or hitomaku-mi, which lasts between one and two hours.

Can't understand the story? Don't fret! Even locals cannot understand the ancient language used in Kabuzi. Rent a headset, and receive an excellent English translation, along with some background information on this treasured art form.

Address: 4-12-15 Ginza, Chuo

Ryogoku Kokugikan (Sumo Wrestling)

Ryogoku, the largest sumo stadium in Japan with a capacity of 10,000 spectators, holds grand tournaments of basho in January, May and September. These magnificent 15-day long tournaments are filled with ceremonies and rituals that are as interesting as the wrestling matches themselves.

The competition begins around 9am each day, with amateur matches, and progress in order of seniority as the day continues. Professional wrestles start around 2:30, but the most exciting match is at 3:50pm, when the top division wrestlers enter the ring.

Tips
English pamphlets for the day's program are available at the stadium. You can also rent radios with live English commentary.

Food inside the stadium is expensive. Food and drink from outside are technically prohibited, but the rule is not always strictly enforced.

Ticket outlets and convenience stores begin selling tickets the month before the match. On the day of the tournament, you can purchase unsold seats from the Kokugikan ticketing box.

Address: 1-3-28, Yokoami, Sumida

Special-themed Cafes and Restaurants

Robot Restaurant
Crazy, amazing, lots of robots fighting lots of pretty girls! The Robot Restaurant offers essentially a cabaret show, Tokyo style. Over dinner, enjoy a riotous time as only the Japanese can cook up.

Address: B2F, 1-7-1 Kabukicho, Shinjuku

Ninja Akasaka

$$$
Ninja Themed Restaurant
Live the life of a ninja! Look for the stealthily place entrance, and navigate through dark corridors across bridges and trap doors to your hidden room, where ninjas serve your meal while performing tricks and illusions. The meal is delicious as well.
Address: Tokyu Hotel Plaza 1F, 2-14-3 Nagata-cho, Akasaka

The Lock Up
Don't be alarmed! To the other side of a long, eerie hallway, is a dungeon-themed izakaya featuring test tube cocktails and gruesomely named food dishes. Tell the staff it's your birthday for an extra special surprise too good to ruin!
Address: B2F Shibuya Grand Tokyo Bldg., 33-1 Udagawacho, Shibuya

Gundam Cafe
This entirely Gundam-themed cafe, features staff dressed in Gundam uniforms, serving robot waffles, cakes, and ice-cream floats.
Address: 1-1 Kandahanaokacho, Chiyoda

AKB48 Cafe
This cafe centers around the 48 hot girls that make up the AKB48.
Address: 4-3-3 Sotokanda, Chiyoda

Neko JaLaLa
At Neko, you can drink tea while stroking the shop's very clean cats.
Address: 3-5-5 Sotokanda, Chiyoda

Cure Maid Cafe
Maid Cafes, where cute girls dress up in maid outfits and dote on their customers, have become a cultural phenomenon across major cities in the world, but of course, they can only have started in Japan. The original inventor of the concept, Cure Maid Cafe is not as over-the-top, or expensive as competitors. Long

lines form here on the weekends for people wanting to experience the original.
Address: 3-15-5 Sotokanda, Chiyoda

MaiDreamin - Heaven's Gate

Here is the best of the maid cafe culture. At MaiDreamin, maids serve tea and other drinks to you, talk to you, and take pictures with you. There are also regular performances on the stage inside.
Address: 3-16-17 Sotokanda Chiyoda

Oedo-Onsen-Monogatari

Tokyo's newest and largest hot spring complex, Oedo-Onsen-Monogatari uses artificially pumped natural groundwater, featuring an endless array of bathtubs of all temperatures and flavors, including inside baths, an outdoor rock bath, a foot bath, and a sand bath. The grounds are decorated in the Edo-era (1800s) style, and offers an authentic Japanese spa experience. There are also plenty of restaurants, bars, souvenir shops, and resting rooms for overnight stays.

Tips
You receive a wrist tag upon entry, which serves as your wallet inside the spa. Charges incurred are paid when you leave.
Entrance fee is expensive, but is discounted after 6pm. There is, however, a late night surcharge after 2am.
Address: 2-57 Aomi, Koto

Akihabara District

Known as Tokyo's "Electric Town", Akihabara offers precisely that - electronics and gadgets of every variety imaginable. Located on the eastern side of central Chiyoda, this district houses thousands of shops selling anything from computers and gaming consoles, to vacuums and DVDs, all at reasonable prices. The area has also become known as the "Gamer's Mecca" in recent times, and associated with Japan's massive anime (cartoon) subculture, with legions of otaku (Japanese for diehard fans) geeks swarming the streets on any given weekend.

Tips
Prices drop as you walk away from the main street, but shops off the beaten path are also less foreigner-friendly.
Bring your passport - Larger shops can arrange immediate sales tax exemptions for purchases over a certain amount.
Remember to check the voltage - Japanese electronics use 100 volts, so you may need a transformer to use them outside Japan.

Ginza District
The glittery streets of Ginza give New York's Fifth Avenue a run for its money. The district is the epicenter of Japan's luxury fashion scene, and home to iconic international brands like Chanel, Louis Vuitton and Christian Dior. But Ginza caters to more than just the super-rich with plenty of affordable shopping and dining options. Those on a budget should stop by the largest flagship store of Uniqlo, a popular and practical Japanese clothing retailer. In addition, you can find Japan's top hotels, like Hotel Monterey and Hotel Seijo, and some of its most famous restaurants in Ginza.

Tips
There are a lot of duty free shopping in Ginza. Be sure to bring your passport!

Karaoke-Kan (Karaoke Chain)
You may have spotted Karaoke-Kan in the film Lost in Translation. This popular Karaoke chain offers rooms for one person to a large party.
Various locations throughout Tokyo

Eats
Tokyo has an eclectic collection of international and local flavors. You can find the most delicious and fresh sushi around Tsukiji Market, enjoy the unique Japanese pub experience at various izakayas, or savor the delicate and beauty-in-the-details kaiseki courses, or Japanese styled tapas. Finally, sample the traditional

sumo wrestler meal, chanko stew, at chanko restaurants in the Ryogoku District. Fret not; the chanko stew is actually quite healthy. Since Tokyo is an epicenter of East Asia's nightlife, you will easily find all sorts of bars and pubs, especially in Shibuya and Shinjuku.

Recommendations:

Umegaoka Sushino Midori Ginza
Japanese, Sushi
$$
Sushi at Umegaoka is known for being generously sized. Like the best sushi places in Tokyo, be prepared to wait for a few hours. Come in groups of two for a shorter wait.
Address: 7-2 Ginza, Chuo

Chanko Tomogata
Japanese
$$
While in the center of the sumo culture, eat like a sumo wrestler! Chanko-nabe is a hearty stew that forms the bulk of a wrestler's diet. Strangely, you shouldn't be concerned with the calories - the stew is chicken, fish, tofu and vegetables cooked in a clear broth. The difference between you and the wrestlers? They can probably down 5 of these, while you should definitely bring at least one friend to share this hearty dish with.
Address: 2-17-6 Ryogoku, Sumida

New York Bar & Grill
Located inside the Park Hyatt, this iconic bar and one of the main sets for the film Lost in Translation is located on the 52nd floor. Kick back in the dark decor, and enjoy stunning views through the floor-to-ceiling windows, while listening to live jazz every night of the week. Bill Murray had a 17-year-old Suntory Hibiki whisky in the film, you can, too!
Address: Park Hyatt Tokyo 52F, 3-7-1-2 Nishishinjuku, Shinjuku

Narisawa
$$$
Japanese, Asian
Narisawa boasts 3 Michelin star, and is one of the best and most innovative restaurants in Tokyo, even in Asia. Be prepared for a highly unusual and delicious feast, and be sure to make a reservation ahead of time.
Address: 2-6-15 Minami Aoyama, Minato

Kobe Beef Kaiseki 511
$$$
Japanese
Here is Japanese barbeque done to perfection. Their dining sets offer as cheap as 1900 yen Japanese beef to premium kobe tenderloin at 14000 yen. The kobe beef is fresh and cook to melt-in-your-mouth perfection, well worth the splurge.
Address: Dear Plaza Akasaka, B1, Akasaka 4-3-28, Minato

Kiji Marunouchi
Japanese, Snack
$
This little place specializes in okonomiyaki, a delicious Japanese omelette that is a must try in Tokyo! English menu is available, and you can pick your favorite filling.
Address: Tokyo Bldg. B1, 2-7-3 Marunouchi, Chiyoda

Andy's Shin Hinomoto
Japanese, Izakaya
$$
Adorable little bar, with great quality small bites to go with your drinks. Small space, so reserve ahead of time!
Address: 2-4-4 Yurakucho, Chiyoda

Menya Musahi
Japanese, Ramen
$

Delicious, well priced dip ramen at Menya Musahi. You order at a machine, then hand your ticket to a waiter. Sit at the bar, and get ready to unbuckle your belt! Go for the large, go ahead, we dare you.
Address: K1 Bldg. 1F, 7-2-6 Nishishinjuku, Shinjuku

Nagi
Japanese, Ramen
$
This tiny restaurant located in a tiny alley offers amazing, big flavored ramen of every variety, all deliciously flavorful!
Address: 1-1-10 Kabukicho, Shinjuku

Shinjuku Kappo Nakajima
Japanese
$
Shinjuku Kappo is one of the cheapest Michelin star restaurants in the world. It's heaven on earth for sardine lovers.
Address: 3-32-5 Shinjuku, Shinjuku

Kisoji Shinjuku
Japanese, Sukiyaki
$$
Sukiyaki and wagyu heaven is located right here in Kisoji. Try this unique Japanese way of cooking, which involves cooking thinly sliced, premium wagyu beef in a shallow layer of boiled water, and dipping in a delicious raw egg sauce.
Address: Shinjuku New Fuji Bldg. 4-6F, 3-17-5 Shinjuku, Shinjuku

Asakusa Okonomiyaki Sometaro
Japanese, Snacks
$
Try out a couple of different fillings for your okonomiyaki, a delicious Japanese omelette, it's the real deal at Sometaro!
Address: 2-2-2 Nishiasakusa, Taito

Irokawa
Japanese
$$
The specialty at Irokawa is unagi, or grilled eel that has been marinated in flavorful sauce. Try it over a bowl of rice.
Address: 2-6-11 Kaminarimon, Taito

Mokushundo
$$
At this traditional restaurant, old-style dishes are cooked tableside on hot lava rocks from Mt. Fuji.
Address: 2-10-8 Sekiguchi, Bunkyo

Gen Yamamoto
It's a tight fit in this tiny bar with just 8 seats, but the mixed drinks will so wow you that you forget to be claustrophobic. Yamamoto, the bartender, takes a connoisseur's approach to his ingredients, explaining the origins of each in Japanese as well as English. With minimal decor and no loud music normally found in a bar, this venue is more like a temple, dedicated to the art of cocktails.
Address: 1-6-4 Azabu-Juban, Minato

Zoetrope
If you are a whisky lover, be sure to drop by Zoetrope for its 300 varieties of Japanese whisky. Not that you should try all 300 at once, but rare bottles like Mercian and the up-and-coming distillery Venture Whisky are sure to make you wish you can head back every night.
Address: 3rd floor, Gaia Building #4, 7-10-14 Nishi Shinjuku, Shinjuku

Popeye Beer Club
Popeye is one of the best places to try Japanese microbrews, with 40 beers on tap from ales to barley wines. English menus are available.
Address: 2-18-7 Ryogoku, Sumida

Where to Stay

Special Places to Stay

Aside from usual hotels and hostels, you can find several uniquely Japanese lodgings. If there is time, add to your Japan experience by trying these out!

Capsule Hotels
With their space shortage, it's no wonder the Japanese came up with capsule hotels, the ultimate in space-efficient sleeping. For a small fee (normally between ¥3,000 and ¥4,000), the guest rents a literal capsule, just enough to lie down. Capsule hotels are segregated by sex, but only a few cater to women.
In Shinjuku and Shibuya districts, capsule hotels are a bit more expensive - at least ¥3,500 - but provide excellent amenities like free massage chairs, saunas, public baths, disposable razors and shampoo, magazines and coffee in the morning.
Tips
On entering a capsule hotel, take off your shoes, place them in a locker, and put on a pair of slippers. On checking in, you will be given a second locker for your belongings.
Sometimes the "door" to your capsule is just a curtain. Beware of probing hands, and bring earplugs to block out snores of tired businessmen.

Ryokan
These traditional Japanese inns are an one-of-a-kind experience. There are two types of ryokans: a small traditional-style inn, with wooden buildings, long verandahs, and gardens; a more modern high-rise that are more like a luxury hotel with fancy public baths. Some ryokans hesitate to take non-Japanese guests, especially those who do not speak Japanese, but some venues especially cater to foreigners. A night for one person with two meals start at

¥8000 and goes up into the stratosphere. ¥50,000 a night per person is not uncommon for some of the posher ones.

Tips
Ryokans usually operate on a strict schedule. You will be expected to arrive by 5PM.

a Ryokan

Love Hotels
"Sex hotel" may be a more accurate term for these establishments. You can find them across Tokyo, though they will usually cluster around highway interchanges or main train stations out of the city - before someone returns home to their family in the suburbs? The entrance is usually discrete, and there is a separate exit to avoid unnecessary run-ins.

The idea is, you rent a room either by the night (listed as "Stay", usually ¥6000-10000) or a few hours ("Rest", usually around ¥3000), or off hours ("No Time Service"). Beware of service

27

charges, peak hour surcharges and taxes, which can bump up your bill by 25%.

Tips

Some love hotels have exotic themes, like aquatics, sports, or Hello Kitty. Rooms feature amenities such as jacuzzis, theme decorations, costumes, karaoke machines, vibrating beds, sex toy vending machines, or even video games. Usually all toiletries (including condoms) are included.

Take some food and drinks with you, since like any hotels, the offerings in mini-fridges have hiked prices.

Love hotels are not a good option for exploring the city, since once you leave, you won't be readmitted. "Stay" rates usually start only after 10PM, and overstaying will incur additional charges.

Recommended Places

Shinjuku District:

Anshin Oyado Shinjuku Ekimae
$
Address: 4-2-10 Shinjuku, Shinjuku
Citadines
$$
Address: 1-2-9 Kabukicho, Shinjuku

Nishitetsu
$$
Address: 7-23-2 Nishi Shinjuku, Shinjuku

Hilton Tokyo
$$$
Address: 6-6-2 Nishishinjuku, Shinjuku

Park Hyatt Tokyo
$$$$
Address: 3-7-1-2 Nishi Shinjuku, Shinjuku

Shibuya Area:

Shibuya Granbell Hotel
$$
Address: 15 - 17 Sakuragaoka-cho, Shibuya

Dormy Inn
$$
Address: 6-24-4 Jingumae, Shibuya

Hotel Century Southern Tower
$$$
Address: 2-2-1 Yoyogi, Shibuya

Cerulean Tower
$$$
Address: 26-1 Sakuragaoka-cho, Shibuya

Ginza District:

Hotel Monterey
$$
Address: 2-10-2 Ginza, Chuo

Mercure Tokyo
$$$
Address: 2-9-4 Ginza, Chuo

Millennium Mitsui Garden Hotel
$$$
Address: 5-11-1 Ginza, Chuo

Akakusa District

Khaosan Tokyo Kabuki
$
Address: 1-17-2 Asakusa, Taito

Hotel Mystays Asakusa
$
Address: 1-5-5 Asakusabashi, Taito

The Gate Hotel Asakusa
$$
Address: 2-16-11 Kaminarimon, Taito

Richmond Hotel Asakusa
$$
Address: 2-7 Asakusa, Taito

Ryokan Kamogawa
$$$
Address: 1-30-10 Asakusa, Taito

Around Tokyo Station

Sotetsu Fresa Inn
$
Address: 2-11-1 Kyobashi, Chuo

Yaesu Terminal
$$
Address: 1-5-14 Yaesu, Chuo

The Tokyo Station Hotel
$$$
Address: 1-9-1 Marunouchi, Chiyoda

Perfect Day Trips from Tokyo

Disney Resort Tokyo

Mt. Fuji

Nikko

KYOTO

In this ancient Japanese *City of Ten Thousand Shrines*, culture, history, and natural beauty come together to compose pieces of stunning art that can only exist here, and nowhere else. Reputedly the most beautiful city in Japan, Kyoto contains 20% of Japan's national treasures, and 14% of its important cultural properties. There are also 17 UNESCO World Heritage Sites in the region.

Located in the center of the Island of Honshu, Kyoto has a population of about 1.5 million. Until 1868, it served as the capital of imperial Japan for more than one thousand years. Today, it is the 7th largest city, and a major part of the Kyoto-Osaka-Kobe metropolitan area, not to mention arguably Japan's most important cultural and historical site.

Kyoto is also one of the few Japanese cities to have escaped allied bombings during World War II. As a result, Kyoto has kept many of its pre-war buildings, such as the traditional townhouses known as *machiya*, no longer found elsewhere. While Kyoto has undergone continuous modernization, and replaced some older buildings with newer architecture, like the Kyoto Station complex, you still come to this city for a taste of its long, epic, and often intriguing story.

If you want to learn, Kyoto will offer to teach you nearly the entirety of Japan's long history. If you are receptive, Kyoto will show you one-of-a-kind landscapes you are not likely to ever forget.

What to See

Kinkaku-ji (Golden Pavilion)
Kiyomizu-dera Temple
Fushimi Inari Shrine
Tenryu-Ji Temple

Sanjusangen-do Temple
Saiho-ji Koke-dera Temple
Arashiyama Bamboo Forest
Iwatayama Monkey Park
Ginkaku-ji (Silver Pavilion)
Nijo Castle
Imperial Park

Kinkaku-ji Temple

Kinkaku-ji Temple
Also known as the Temple of the Golden Pavilion, Kinkaku-ji is the most popular tourist attraction in Kyoto. It was originally built in the late 14th century as a retirement villa for Shogun Ashikaga Yoshimitsu, and later converted into a temple. The beautiful vista and the reflection of the luminous temple on the water makes for a striking photo - if you can keep the mobs of tourists out of it. Visit early to avoid the tour groups.
Address: 1 Kinkakuji-cho, Kita-ku, Kyoto

Kyomizu-dera Temple

Incredible views of the city from the temple complex's elevated main hall, which has a wooden veranda supported by hundreds of pillars, is Kyomizu-dera's major attraction. But you can also stop by the love-themed Jishu Shrine, and purchase a charm to help win the affections of the one you love, or walk with your eyes closed between the "love stones" positioned 18 meters apart, to confirm your loved one's affection. There is also the waterfall, under which you can stand and collect water to drink with a little tin cup. Lastly, if you are up for a workout, take the path that leads into the mountain and take in the lovely forest and green scenery.

Address: 1-294 Kiyomizu, Higashiyama-ku, Kyoto

Fushimi Inari Shrine

Very often overlooked in the midst of Kyoto's countless temples, this jewel of a shrine is dedicated to Inari, Japan's fox goddess, and the head shrine for 40,000 Inari shrines across Japan. Walk up the hillside through the bright red torii gates, and take in the city from this elevated vantage point. Admission is free.

Address: 68 Fukakusa Yabunouchicho, Fushimi-ku, Kyoto

Fushimi Inari Shrine

Tenryu-ji Temple
Considered one of Kyoto's five Great Zen Temples, Tenryu-ji Temple is a UNESCO World Heritage Site and the main temple of the Rinzai sect of Buddhism in Kyoto. The original temple building dates back to the 14th century, but the current is a reconstruction from the last century. Do take a leisurely stroll around the lovely garden and pond, both designed by Zen master Musō Soseki. Afterwards, exit through the north gate, walk through the splendid bamboo forest to reach the Ōkōchi Sansō villa.
Address: 68 Saga Tenryuji Susukinobabacho, Ukyo-ku, Kyoto

Sanjusangen-do
From the street, this walled compound does not look like much. But once inside this ancient temple dating back to 1164, you will find a peaceful and spiritual place, with 1001 beautiful wooden and gold-leaf covered statues of Kannon, the Buddhist goddess of mercy, housed in 33 bays in the main hall. Afterwards, stroll in

the garden and splash your face with refreshing spring water, and take a minute to meditate in the tranquility.
Address: 657 Sanjusangendo Mawaricho, Kyoto

Saiho-ji Koke-dera Temple
Also known as Saiho-ji, Kokedera is a World Heritage Sites famous for its beautiful moss garden. Visit in summer or autumn, when the garden is at the height of its beauty.

Unlike other temples, Kokedera has a strict reservation process in order to limit the number of visitors, and avoid having too many people step on and kill the moss. At least one week prior to your visit, preferably at least three, you should send a letter giving your name, the number of people in your party, and the dates you prefer to visit along with a self-addressed stamped envelope, at Saiho-ji Temple, 56 Jingatani-cho, Matsuo Nishikyo-ku, Kyoto, 615-8286, Japan.

If you are in Japan already, request an "ofuku hagaki". If outside Japan, you can request an International Reply Coupon (IRC) to cover the postage. The temple will let you know whether you have been accepted, and what day and time you have been scheduled. You'll want to be flexible in your schedule as the temple may suggest a day earlier or later. Be very punctual, otherwise you will be denied entry.

Tip
If accepted, you will pay 3,000 yen upon admission. The ticket includes listening to a monk recite sutras, which is quite an experience, but does require you to sit on your legs or crosslegged for nearly an hour. Request a low chair if you think sitting on the floor will be a problem for you.

Address: 56 Matsuo Jingatanicho, Nishikyo-ku, Kyoto

Arashiyama Bamboo Forest
The beautiful bamboo forest is one of the most photographed sights in Kyoto, but no picture can do justice to the sense of

wonder you feel standing in the midst of this sprawling bamboo grove. It is unlike any forests you may have seen before.

Iwatayama Monkey Park
When you have gotten enough of temples and shrines in the city, take some time off to feed the macaque monkeys in this park. Don't bring food with you - the monkeys prefer the peanuts on sale inside the shack on top of the mountain inside the park. They also seem fond of the keeper's motorcycle, which is usually parked next to the shack.
Address: 8 Genrokuyamacho, Nishikyo-ku, Kyoto

Ginkaku-ji
Situated at the northern end of the Philosopher's Walk, Ginkaku, also known as the Silver Pavilion, is a popular spot with tourists that can get very crowded. The temple was built in 1482 by Shogun Ashikaga Yoshimasa, who modeled this retirement villa after his grandfather's retirement villa - Kinkaku-ji, the Golden Pavilion at the base of the northern mountains.

Most stroll through the dry Zen garden and the surrounding moss garden (a must-see!), before posing for pictures in front of the pavilion across a pond.
Address: 2 Ginkakuji-cho Sakyo-ku, Kyoto

Nijo Castle
Nijo Castle, the one-time power center of the imperial regime, is now one of the most noteworthy highlights of Kyoto. This complex, with its tastefully curated gardens and splendid centuries-old structures, was the official Kyoto residence of the "shogun", or the head of defense of imperial Japan, dating back to the 1600's.
The grounds consist of two concentric rings of fortifications, the Ninomaru Palace, the ruins of the Honmaru Palace, various support buildings and several gardens. Pay special attention to the series of ornately-decorated reception rooms within the Ninomaru Palace, with its famous "nightingale floor" - the intricate wooden

flooring makes bird-like squeaking sounds when stepped on, to give advance warning when someone is approaching.

Rent an audio guide in English at the front entrance if you want to learn more about the rich history of the castle. Most signs are also in English.

Tip
Avoid the early morning hours, when tour groups flood the place. Late morning or lunch hour would be a much better choice. If possible, also avoid the summer, when Japanese school children are taken to these historical sites in hoards.
Address: 541 Nijojo-cho, Horikawa-nishiiru, Kyoto

Imperial Park
This sprawling and peaceful complex in the center of Kyoto, contains the Kyoto Imperial Palace, the Sento Imperial Palace, and vast grounds home to 50,000 trees, including cherry, plum, and peach tree orchards.

Kyoto Imperial Palace is a reconstruction of the original, dating from 1855. Although the current imperial family does not actually spend much time here, it nonetheless provides interesting insight into the lives of the imperial court.

Sento Imperial Palace, or Sento Gosho, served as the residence of retired emperors during the Edo era. Today, Sento is essentially a private park within the larger palace complex. There is a guided tour, but you may wish to just hang out and soak in the peaceful green splendor of the place that will make you forget all about the bustles of the city outside.
Address: 3 Kyoto-Gyoen Kamigyo-ku, Kyoto 602-0881, Kyoto

Experiences

Take the Philosopher's Walk
Take a riverboat cruise down Hozu River

Walking tour in the Gion Geisha District
Zen meditation
Hitch a rickshaw ride

Philosopher's Walk
This scenic pedestrian path follows a cherry-tree-lined canal between Ginkaku-ji (Silver Pavilion) and Nanzen-ji, a Meiji-era temple. The route is named after the influential 20th century Japanese philosopher and Kyoto University professor Nishida Kitaro, who is thought to have strolled the path daily for meditation. Along the way, you will find a number of Kyoto's best temples, including Hōnen-in, Ōtoyo Shrine, and Eikan-dō Zenrin-ji. The beautiful walk will take about 30 minutes, but most people spend more time visiting the majestic temples along the way. During the cherry blossom season, or the fall when the leaves are changing color, you'll be hard pressed to find a prettier (or a more crowded, probably) walk anywhere else.

Hozu River Cruise
Catch a boat ride down the Hozu River, so you can experience Arashiyama to the fullest. You will find boats waiting on either side of the river, but confirm how far and for how long the trip goes. Cruises range between 20 minutes to two hours. Be prepared to get splashed, and dress appropriately.
Address: 2 Shimonakajima Hozucho, Kameoka 621-0005, Kyoto

Gion Geisha District
Walk the flagstone-paved streets between traditional buildings of the Gion district, and watch real-life geishas hurry past you. Here in Gion District, the geisha culture is very much alive. The area just north of Shijo-dori, to the west of Yasaka Shrine, is especially photogenic,, especially around the two streets called Shinbashi-dori and Hanami-koji. The two sloping streets, Sannen-zaka and Ninen-zaka, are also great for pictures. Around 6pm or 9pm are good times to spot a geisha, as they will be leaving their boarding houses then. But please remember to be respectful - you don't

want to be the obnoxious tourist chasing a poor girl for a picture, as they walk away as fast as possible.

Geishas

Geisha Walking Tour and Lecture
If you wanted to learn more about the exotic world of the Geisha, be sure to book a walking lecture, which includes entrance into a teahouse, a history lesson of the unique geisha culture, and numerous photo opportunities along the walk in the Gion district.

You can book here:
http://www.kyotosightsandnights.com/walking.html, for ¥3,000 per person.

Zen meditation
There is no better place to try Zen meditation than in the ancient temples of Kyoto.

Shuko-in
The vice abbot at Shuko-in, Taka Kawakami, is American-educated. He leads a detailed English tour of the temple, and its Zen meditation lessons. The temple also hosts many important artistic and cultural properties related to Zen, with connections to Shinto and Christianity. Find more information here: http://www.shunkoin.com/.
Address: 42 Myoshiji-cho, Hanazono, Ukyo-ku, Kyoto

Taizo-in
Aside from a one-hour long meditation session, visitors are also treated to a brief tea ceremony, calligraphy lessons, and an English tour of the temple's garden. While you will need to make reservations at their website (http://www.taizoin.com/en/), and dedicate half a day to the session, the experience is a once-in-a-lifetime opportunity. Participants must be at least 15 years of age, so don't take the kids!
Address: Address: 35 Hanazono Myoshinjicho, Ukyo-ku, Kyoto

Rickshaw Ride
Forget what you've seen in Hollywood films of poor, destitute rickshaw pullers. Kyoto's modern day rickshaw pullers are more

than a cheap transport option, they are also knowledgeable tour guides eager to show you another side of the city. The men pulling today are highly regarded for keeping this cultural element alive, and often highly attractive. Some of the most popular pullers even have regular patrons.

Eats
With so many shrines and temples, Buddhist monks' simple fares have been elevated to an art form in Kyoto - try **Shigetsu** for an immersive and beautiful experience, or specialty tofu at **Yudofuya Restaurant**. After tea ceremonies, try something more down to earth at **Kasagiya**, which specializes in tea and local desserts. **Nishiki Market**, known as "Kyoto's Pantry" offers plenty of traditional snacks you can walk and eat. For a splurge, look no further than premium wagyu beef, at **Otsuka**.

Around Central Kyoto

Nishiki Market
Literally named the "brocade market", Nishiki Market is known to locals as "Kyoto's Pantry", as it is easily the best traditional food market in the city. You'll find all the major ingredients of traditional Kyoto cuisine here: tsukemono (Japanese pickles), fresh tofu, Kyo-yasai (Kyoto's specialty vegetables), wagashi (Japanese sweets), tea, and fresh fish and shellfish. You can also eat as you go - sample from stalls peddling yakitori (meat cooked on skewers) and sashimi - or sit down at a restaurant found amid the shops. You might even score some exotic whale meat if you are lucky!
Location: Nishikikoji-dori, Nakagyo-ku (between Teramachi and Takakura)

Sashimi

Pontocho Area
Take a night stroll down this narrow lane running from Shijo-dori to Sanjo-dori, one block west of the Kamo River. Pontocho is one of the Kyoto's most traditional nightlife districts. You'll find anything from super-exclusive geisha houses to common yakitori bars.

Tip
Feel free to visit any establishment with a menu and listed prices. Avoid others to be safe.

Chao Chao Sanjo Kiyamachi
$
Japanese
Kick back with some pork or shrimp gyoza, pan-fried dumplings, and good drinks. For dessert, try the chocolate gyoza with ice cream.

Address: 117 Ishiyacho Kiya-Machi Sanjo Kudaru Nakagyo-Ku,Kyoto

Demachi Futaba
$
Japanese, Dessert
Try one, or several, of the great variety of red bean based Japanese dessert at this store.
Address: 236 Seiryucho, Kamigyo-ku, Kyoto 602-0822

Menbakaichidai
$$
Japanese, Noodles
Sit at the bar, and chat with the father and son team at Menbakaichidai as they prepare your bowl of ramen. Order the "fire ramen" for a little surprise show.
Address: 757-2 Minamiiseyacho Kamigyo-Ku, Kyoto 602-8153

Hafuu Honten
$$$
Japanese and French Fusion
Prepare for the best steak of your life! This Japanese and French fusion restaurant is a little out of the way in Kyoto's Central district, but is by all accounts, worth the short hike. The headliner here at Hafuu Honten is premium wagyu beef - stewed, thinly-sliced, grilled, and every other way, all of them incredible. There are also plenty of good wine and delicious desserts to round out what many claim will be, the absolute best meal of your trip to Japan.
Address: 471-1 Sasayacho, Nakagyo-ku, Kyoto 604-0983

Yoshikawa Inn Tempura
$$$$
Japanese, Tempura
If you are going to splurge on one meal, make it here. Forget what tempura you've had at the Japanese restaurant back home, because they hardly deserve the name next to Yoshikawa's

offerings. Sit at the bar and watch the chef work his magic on the freshest ingredients, perfectly fried.
Address: 135 Matsushitacho, Tominokojidori Oike-sagaru, Nakagyo-ku, Kyoto 604-8093

Around Western Kyoto

Shigetsu
$$$
Japanese, Vegetarian
Shigetsu will show you what "vegetarian" really means. Sitting on the ground of this temple garden, you will be served delicate dishes that are the traditional fares of the monks in Kyoto, including tofu, which is a regional specialty.
Address: 68 Sagatenryujisusukinobabacho, Tenryuji Temple, Ukyo-ku, Kyoto 616-8385

Otsuka
$$$
Japanese, Steakhouse
Great place to sample wagyu beef. Like other steakhouses serving this premium cut, Otsuka is a little expensive, running between 3,500 yen to 6,000 yen for a set meal. But you know that your food will arrive perfectly cooked.
Address: 20-10 Sagatenryuji Setogawacho, Ukyo-ku, Kyoto 616-8376

Hirokawa
$$
Japanese
You are here for eel, or in Japanese, unagi. At Hirokawa, that unagi comes perfectly grilled, lightly-coated in sauce, served over rice. Yum!
Address: Sagatenryujikitatsukurimichicho, Ukyoku, Kyoto 616-8374

Around Eastern Kyoto

Kasagiya
$
Tea
Between temples, drop by this little traditional tea shop for a cup of Japanese matcha and snack on sweet glutinous riceballs.
Address: 349 Masuyacho Higashiyamaku, Kyoto 605-0826

Arabica Kyoto
$
Coffee
Amazing cup of coffee situated between the temples.
Address: 87-5 Hoshinocho, Higashiyama-ku, Kyoto 605-0853

Senmonten
$
Chinese
Great place to relax, grab a beer, and some incredible pan-fried dumplings.
Address: Higashiyama-ku | Higashi-gawa, Hanamikoji Shimbashi kudaru, Kyoto 605-0084

Karako
$$
Japanese, Noodles
Karako specializes in cheap and comforting food, specifically, ramen noodles and fried chicken.
Address: 12-3 Okazaki Tokuseicho, Sakyo-ku, Kyoto 606-8351

Okariba
$$$
Japanese
Try out the most tender boar, trout, and other grilled delicacies while the owner of Okariba regales you with his wild hunting stories.
Address: 43-3 Okazaki Higashitenno-cho, Sakyo-ku | Residence Okazaki 1F, Kyoto

Hyotei
$$$$
Japanese
It's hard to say which is more beautiful - the food at Hyotei, or the vista. This three Michelin star restaurant serves its exquisite small dishes, "kaiseki" style, in individual rooms situated in a stunning ancient garden.
Address: Nanzenjikusagawacho, Sakyoku, Kyoto 606-8437

Northern Kyoto

Yudofuya Restaurant
$$
Japanese
Situated within the Ryoan-ji Temple is this delightful little tofu restaurant. You sit in a quiet room on tatami mats, and savor the special tofu hot pot and vegetarian lunch, while looking out to the exquisite garden with a tranquil pond. Speak in whispers only, to avoid disturbing the ambience.
Address: 13 Ryoanji Goryonoshitacho, Kyoto

Kurazushi
$
Sushi
Kurazushi serves "conveyor belt" sushi. At 100 yen a plate, each holding 2 pieces of sushi, this place is a steal. That doesn't mean the sushi is not fresh though, because as soon as each plate is placed on the conveyor, a hungry patron snatches it right up.
Address: 4 Hirano Miyajikicho Kita-ku, Kyoto 603-8365

Where to Stay

Kyoto boasts some of the most extraordinary ryokans. These traditional Japanese inns are an one-of-a-kind experience and if you didn't get to stay in one while in Tokyo, don't miss it in Kyoto. There are two types of ryokans: a small traditional-style inn, with wooden buildings, long verandahs, and gardens; a more modern high-rise that are more like a luxury hotel with fancy public baths.

Again, some ryokans hesitate to take non-Japanese guests, especially those who do not speak Japanese, but some venues especially cater to foreigners. A night for one person with two meals start at ¥8,000 and goes up into the stratosphere. ¥50,000 a night per person is not uncommon for some of the posher ones.
Arguably the best ryokans in Japan can be found right here in the Higashiyama area. Listed below are the best of the best, famous for their hospitality, attention to detail, and truly authentic experiences.

Shiraume
Proprietor Tomoko of Shiraume is known for her thoughtful touches, delicious meals, and great stories about the ryokan and the history of Kyoto.
Address: Shirakawa-hotori, Shinbashi-dori, Gionmachi, Higashiyama-ku, Kyoto

Hotel Mume
Hidden behind a red door in the geisha district, Mume offers a great happy hour, excellent services and reservations at local restaurants that you'd never find on your own.
Address: 261 Shinmonzen dori, Umemotocho, Higashiyama-ku

Ohanabo
A great mid-range ryokan, Ohanabo serves a great kaiseki style dinner in your room, and breakfast in a common room. There is also a hot spring, and yukatas for everyone to wear!
Address: 66-2 Shokuyacho, Shimojuzuyamachi Agaru, Akezudori, Shimogyo-ku | Higashihonganji, Kyoto

Salon Haraguchi Tenseian

This tranquil hotel is located in the middle of Maruyama Park. The owners have a couple of bikes on hand for you to borrow, in case you wanted to explore the city that way.
Address: 7-3 Maruyama-cho, higashiyama-ku, Kyoto

Motonago
Unlike many modernized ryokans, Motonago is the real deal. The bathroom is shared, but you can book it for certain hours to have it for yourself.
Address: 511 Washio-cho, Higashiyama-ku | Nene no Michi, Kyoto

Hiiragya
A bit pricier than the rest, but well worth the splurge. Ask for one of the old rooms next to the garden, and you may not want to leave.
Address: 277 Nakahakusancho, Huyacho Anekoji-agaru, Nakagyo-ku, Kyoto

Ryokan Shimizu
Only 10-15 minutes from Kyoto Station, Shimizu is perfectly situated, and comes with impeccable customer service.
Address: 646 Kagiya-cho, Shimogyo-ku, Kyoto

Maifukan
Great service, and you can choose from western and Japanese style rooms at Maifukan.
Address: Minamimonmae Yasakajinja Gion Higashiyama-ku, Kyoto

Arashiyama Benkei
Many rooms of this ryokan in Arashiyama face the lake. It is also only a short walk from the stunning bamboo forest.
Address: 34 Sagatenryuji Susukinobabacho Ukyo-ku, Kyoto

Perfect Day Trips

Uji
Himeji

UJI

Take a quick detour to Uji from Kyoto, and see historical Japan as it has been for thousands of years, almost entirely unencumbered the developments of modernity. With a history as long as as that of its more famous neighbor, the ancient city of Uji has retained even more of its old-world charms than Kyoto. It is the scene of many famous Japanese stories, including the final chapters of the Tale of Genji, Japan's first novel. There are stores in this city that have been open for hundreds of years, and several important temples less trodden by Kyoto's hoards of tourists. Uji is also the tea capital of Japan, so be sure to partake in the many activities surrounding this culture.

Getting There

Uji is on the JR Nara Line. From Kyoto Station, it is just 17 minutes away via rapid train, or 27 minutes via local. The ticket costs ¥230.

You will arrive at the JR Uji station. There is a small tourist information center just outside, where you can grab a English map. Most sights are around here too, so just walk along the river while you are in Uji, and you will hit all the important spots!

See

Byōdō-in Temple
Byōdō-in was built in 1053, by Fujiwara Yorimichi, a chief advisor to the emperor. Originally a villa constructed by his

father, Fujiwara converted Byōdō-in into a temple in anticipation of the coming of a dark age where Buddhism would disappear. Since its establishment, this temple became a refuge for the faithful during many stretches of history, and gave rise to the Pure Land Faith movement of Buddhism.

You can walk around the grounds, and check out the museum that holds many of the temple's ancient artifacts. Unfortunately, the Phoenix Hall, the main structure of the temple - a picture of which is on the ¥10 coin - is under construction for 2015, so you won't be able to take the tour normally offered there.
Address: Renge-116, Uji, 611-0021

Byodo-in Temple

Ujigami Shrine
This modest little shrine is a World Heritage Site, and said to be the oldest Shinto shrine in Japan.
Address: 59 Uji Yamada, Uji 611-0021

Mimurotoji Temple
A great temple to visit for those who love flowers. There are flowers all over the mountainside and throughout the path in the garden, as well as beautiful lotus flowers planted in pots.
Address: 21 Todo Shigatani, Uji 611-0013

Taiho-an Tea House
There is no better place to experience a traditional Japanese tea ceremony than here in the tea capital of Japan. Taiho-an is operated by the government, this tea house right next to *Byōdō-in Temple* has both smaller, authentic tea rooms, and a larger room with a more relaxed atmosphere.
Address: 1-5 Uji, Togawa, Uji

HIMEJI

Located on the western edge of the Kansai region, Himeji is home to Japan's finest castle, the Himeji Castle. This splendid complex has been featured in many films about Japan, including The Last Samurai featuring Tom Cruise.

Getting There

The Hikari train, free of charge to Japan Rail Pass holders, gets you from Kyoto to Himeji in under an hour.

Once there, the castle and other important sights are only a ten to fifteen minute walk from the train station down Otemae-dōri street. Alternatively, you can take the sightseeing loop bus which only costs ¥100, and gets you to the castle in five minutes.

See

Himeji Castle

Also known as the "White Egret Castle", this shimmery white edifice on towering over the city of Himeji was built in the 1300's, and was once the biggest castle in all of Asia. Considered one of the most beautiful castles in Japan, it has luckily eluded the ravages of civil war, natural disasters, and the bombings of World War II.

Himeji Castle

Admission to Himeji is ¥1,000 adults and ¥300 children. A special combination ticket gets you into both the castle and the nearby Kōkoen Garden. There is a free guided tour in English, but only if a guide is available. Please note that since the castle reopened in March 2015 after several years of renovation, the number of visitors have soared. Go early, and expect to spend a few hours waiting in line. Avoid holidays and weekends if possible!
Address: 68 Hommachi, Himeji 670-0012

Kokoen Garden
Located next to Himeji Castle's outer moat, this magnificent collection of nine Edo-style walled gardens were laid out in 1992 on the site of ancient samurai houses. The gated partitions are faithful to the ruins of residential quarters, but within each enclosure, landscaped gardens and water features have been established in place of the noble houses. There is also a tea arbor and a restaurant.
Address: 68 Honmachi, Himeji 670-0012

Engyo-ji Temple
You'll have to take the orange bus No. 8 from Himeji Castle for 30 minutes to reach Engyo-ji Temple, located in Mt. Shosha, but fans of Tom Cruise's *The Last Samurai* will not want to miss this beautiful temple, which served as the setting for the film. It is particularly in the fall, when the Japanese maples change color.
Address: 2968 Shosha, Himeji 671-2201

OSAKA

Osaka is, and has been many things. Dating back to the Asuka period in 500AD, it is one of Japan's oldest cities and its one-time capital. Even after the imperial capital moved elsewhere, Osaka continued to serve as a hub for land, sea, and river-canal transportation and commerce. In the Tokugawa era, the city emerged as the "Nation's Kitchen", the collection and distribution point for rice. During the Meiji era, Osaka's entrepreneurs led the country in industrial development. Bombing during World War II nearly obliterated this long historical heritage. After which, the city underwent a thorough, rapid, and by Japan's exacting standards, inelegant modern day reconstruction.

Today, Osaka is the third largest city in the country with a population of 3 million, and is known for its gruff appearance - even the ancient castle is a concrete reconstruction - and its open, brash, and above all, very funny inhabitants. Osaka is also acknowledged as Japan's best place to eat, drink, and party, beating out even Tokyo. Consider visiting Osaka before or after Kyoto - after days of temple hopping, Zen meditating, and nature gazing, you're sure to love all the modern fun Osaka has to offer!

Recommended Stay: 1-2 Days

Osaka

What to See

<u>Osaka Castle</u>
While this post-WWII reconstruction of the original Osaka Castle pales in comparison with other magnificent castles Japan has to offer, like Himeiji Castle, it is still a popular destination for its huge collection of historical artifacts of the Osaka area. In the spring, Osakans also love going to the castle's vast park for cherry blossom viewing and a picnic.
Address: 1-1 Osakajo, Chuo-ku, Osaka

<u>Osaka Kaiyukan Aquarium</u>
One of the largest public aquariums in the world and Osaka's most popular destination, Osaka Kaiyukan attracts huge crowds with its walk-through displays of marine life. Those traveling with children won't want to miss this! After spending a few hours learning about the sea, enjoy a ride on the 112.5 meter high Tempozan Ferris Wheel, for a panoramic view of the whole city.

Address: 1-1-10 Kaigan-dori, Minato-ku, Osaka

Umeda Sky Building
Built in the late 1980s, the Umeda Sky Building was originally envisioned as a "City of Air" in the form of four huge, interconnected towers. In the end, the city ended up with a 40-story, 173-meter building that, being so strangely shaped, has become one of Osaka's most recognizable landmarks. While offices occupy most of the 40 stories, there are markets and restaurants underground, and a rooftop observatory with an impressive view. The observatory is popular with Osaka's lovers - you can sit in a special seat with your loved one, each press a metal button to light up the ground around you into a heart. YOu can also purchase an engraved heart love for the padlock wall around the seat.
Address: 1-1-88 Oyodonaka, Kita-ku, Osaka 531-0076

Sumiyoshi Taisha Shrine
This Shinto shrine, one of Japan's oldest dating back to the 3rd century, is dedicated to three gods that protect the nation, sea voyages, and for promoting waka (31-syllable) poetry. The beautiful Sorihashi Bridge leads to the entrance of the main shrine grounds, and creats a uniquely high arch over a pond of black turtles.
Address: 2-9-89 Sumiyoshi, Sumiyoshi-ku, Osaka

Shitenno-ji Temple
This large, tranquil temple provides a bit of serenity in the bustling and loud city of Osaka. Originally built in 593 AD, what you see currently is a post-WWII reconstruction. Walk around the main hall and the garden, and if you'd like, pay to go into the pagoda that has many primitive Japanese Buddhist wall paintings.
Address: 1-11-18 Shitennoji, Tennoji-ku, Osaka

Universal Studios Japan
Rather like its American counterpart, Universal Studios Japan is a huge theme park inspired by blockbuster Hollywood movies.

Address: 2-1-33 Sakurajima, Konohana-ku, Osaka

Experiences

National Bunraku Theater
This is one of the last places in the world where you can still watch bunraku, an intricate form of puppet theater originating from the Edo period. Each of the puppets require three operators. Great Japanese plays of the 1600s and 1700s are accompanied by traditional music and narration. English synopses of the script are provided.
Address: 1-12-10 Nippombashi, Chuo-ku, Osaka

Spa World Complex
The massive Spa World complex in central Osaka is a blend of Japanese baths, Epcot Center, and Las Vegas. In the "European Spa" zone, you'll find themed baths in the styles of Ancient Rome, Greece, Finland, and Atlantis, while in the "Asia Spa" zone, you can bath in Persian and Bali-style pools. There is also a gym, an amusement pool, a stone spa, a salon, a restaurant, and a hotel. You can stay there all day for just ¥2,700!
Address: 3-4-24 Ebisu-higashi, Naniwa-ku, Osaka

Dotonburi Neighborhood
Looking for a fun time and not sure where to go? Just get to Dotonburi, and you'll be all set. The area is named for the Dotonbori Canal, and offers plenty of places to play, eat, drink, shop, and sleep. You wouldn't believe the number of arcades, restaurants, amusement facilities, and people!
Address: Chuo-ku, Osaka

Umeda District
Spending your evening in Umeda is a good bet. You can find every variety of international cuisine here, as well as all the after dinner drinks you can gulp down.

Nightlife in Namba

After Umeda, move to Namba, where Osaka's best clubs (or worst, depending on which you prefer) can be found.. These clubs are open every night of the week, note that they do close around 1am during weekdays. On the weekends, you are free to party all night long!

Eats

Once the rice trading hub of the country, today's Osaka is a gourmand's paradise. Try **okonomiyaki** - the omelet pancake with customizeable filling of your choice. You can find it elsewhere, but it won't be as good as Osaka. Other Osaka staples include **kitsune udon**, thick noodle soup blanketed by fried tofu, and **hakozushi**, sushi pressed flat in a bamboo box. On the street, try out **takoyaki**, ball-shaped octopus fritters. The most adventurous food lover can try **tessa**, sashimi made from poisonous globefish. Certified chefs are trained to leave just a bit of poison to numb your lips, but not enough to stop your heart. Go ahead, take a bite!

HIROSHIMA

Hiroshima became more recognized in the west on the morning of August 6, 1945, when the U.S. Air forces dropped an atomic bomb on the city, near the end of World War II. Since that unfortunate day, however, Hiroshima has been declared a city of peace, and the city government continues to advocate the abolition of all nuclear weapons. Today, it is an industrial city of wide boulevards and criss-crossing rivers, with an excellent food scene and a bustling nightlife.

See

Hiroshima Peace Memorial Park
You will find most of the atomic bombing memorials in the Peace Memorial Park, the target of the bomb, or the areas surrounding it. The park is situated on the site of the busy Nakajima merchant district, which was completed destroyed. Today, there are more than 50 memorials, statues, and other commemorating structures in the park. Some may be obscure in meaning, others devastating. There is no entry fee for the park.
Address: 1 Nakajima-cho, Naka

Hiroshima Peace Memorial Museum
Located on park grounds, the Hiroshima Peace Memorial Museum documents the atomic bomb, and its heart-wrenching aftermath, with scale models of the city's "before" and "after", to melted children's bikes and other displays related to the devastating attack. Please note that some visitors may find the exhibits too graphic. The rest of the museum is devoted to appealing for the abolition of nuclear weapons in the world today, one of the city's biggest initiatives. Note that while we recommend a visit to the museum, you may need some time to decompress after this powerful but disturbing experience.
Address: 1-2 Nakajima-cho, Naka

Hiroshima National Peace Memorial Hall
Also located in the park, the Hiroshima National Peace Memorial Hall collects the names and photographs of people who died in the atomic attack, with a set of kiosks displaying the stories and recollections of the survivors, and a quiet hall of contemplation and respect.
Address: 1-6 Nakajima-chō, Naka-ku

Atomic Bomb Dome
Prior to World War II, Atomic Bomb Dome was one of the most recognizable landmarks of the city, serving as the Hiroshima Prefectural Commercial Exhibition Hall. By sheer chance, the atomic took place almost directly above the dome, which left its walls largely intact while the dome at the top of the building shattered and the people inside were killed. The skeletal remains survived to today. It has become the symbol for Hiroshima, and was declared a World Heritage site in 1996 amid some controversy.
Address: 1-10 Otemachi, Naka

Children's Peace Monument
This monument is dedicated to all the children who died from the impact of the atomic bomb and its aftermath. There is a bronze crane, which is a symbol of peace, underneath the monument. Thousands of paper folded cranes from around the world are also offered around the monument.
Address: 1 Nakajimacho, Naka

The Cenotaph
The Cenotaph contains a stone chest with a registry of the names of every known person who died from the bombing, regardless of nationality. The inscription in Japanese reads, "Let all the souls here rest in peace, for the evil shall not be repeated."
Address: 1 Nakajima-cho, Naka

Peace Bell

The Peace Bell displays an engraving of the world, without borders, to symbolize unity. The public is welcome to strike the bell, which hits on an atomic symbol.
Address: 1 Nakajima-cho, Naka

Chuo Park Area

This big, sprawling green space is where Hiroshima's most athletic congregate, and contains many of the pleasant sights below. With long walking paths and athletic fields, Chuo Park is a pleasant in which to take a stroll, or join an open-invitation soccer, football, and ultimate frisbee match. Don't be shy!

Hiroshima Castle

Built originally in the 1590s by the warlord Terumoto Mori, Hiroshima Castle predates the city itself. After it was destroyed during the war, it was reconstructed in 1958. Today, it offers a nice place to walk, and the locals' favorite place for cherry blossom viewing for its more than 350 cherry trees. The castle contains a museum, with interesting relics and armor from the city's long history. The view from the top is worth the entrance fee alone.
Address: 21-1 Moto-machi, Naka

Hiroshima Museum of Art

Dedicated to European art from late Romanticism to early Picasso, Hiroshima Museum of Art boasts of at least one painting by every famous artist of the period. While none of the works is a major piece that the casual tourist will recognize, it's definitely worth a quick visit.
Address: 3-2 Motomachi, Naka

Shukkei-en Garden

Come to this beautifully landscaped Japanese garden and allow your emotions to settle after the atomic bomb memorials. Wander through the paths, cross ponds on bridges and visit the graceful teahouses and waterfalls.
Address: 2-11 Kaminobori-cho, Naka

Day Trip to Miyajima (See below)

Experiences

Sake Festival

If you are in town in early October, visit the suburb of Saijo, which is just a few train stops from Hiroshima, for an annual sake festival. For the price of entry, you can drink your fill of sake from local breweries. It's a great party of public drunkenness! Outside the festival area, you can also take tours of the breweries, and purchase wooden sake cups among other souvenirs.

Flower Festival

During the first weekend of May, hit up the Flower Festival, Hiroshima's biggest festival first begun in 1975 to celebrate the Carp's first baseball championship. You'll find tons of food vendors, boutique stands, live performances with comedians and Japanese pop bands on stage. The small local bands might be the best, however, you just might discover a diamond in the rough.

Shimizu Gekijo Theater

You'll get a taste of classical Japanese drama, crossed with classical bondage porn. For what it is, the show is mostly tastefully put together. You might see quite a few olden women giving an extravagant tip. While the shows are only in Japanese, the elaborate costumes and make-up are a spectacle in themselves.

Eat

Okonomiyaki

Don't miss Hiroshima's signature dish, Okonomiyaki, while you are here. Aptly named "cook it as you like it", and somewhat misleadingly nicknamed "Japanese pizza", okonomiyaki is a savory pancake made with eggs, cabbage, soba noodles, and fillings like meat, seafood, or cheese. It is grilled in layers in front of you, and drenched in the tasty okonomiyaki sauce. You can also add mayonnaise, pickled ginger, or seaweed to your taste.

The city of Osaka offers a competing type of okonomiyaki. The difference is, in Hiroshima, the ingredients are cooked in layers and pressed together at the end of the cooking process, while in Osaka, the batter is mixed first, and the ingredients do not include soba noodles. If you bring this topic up with a local in Hiroshima, you'd better be prepared to state your preference (Friendly reminder: you are in Hiroshima)!

There are hundreds of okonomiyaki shops in the city, but try Okonomiyaki Village, with more than 25 stalls all selling this delicious snack in one building.
Address: 5-13 Shintenchi, Naka

Oysters
Hiroshima oysters are renowned for being very big and fleshy. Between October and March is the height of Hiroshima's famous oyster season. Try Kanawa Oyster Boat on the river.
Address: 3 Otemachi, Naka

Drink

For a lively nightlife, head to Nagarekawa district, which has the highest concentration of bars in the city, from quieter wine bars on Hakushima-dori, to expats' favorite pubs clustered around the PARCO building. Yagenbori-dori has some multi-level clubs for later in the night.

Perfect Day Trips
Miyajima

MIYAJIMA (Itsukushima)

Itsukushima Shrine

Located off the coast of Hiroshima, the island of Itsukushima offers one of the finest views of Japan. This little island first came on the scene in 806 AD, when the monk Kobo Daishi ascended Mt. Misen and established the mountain as an ascetic site for the Shingon sect of Buddhism. Ever since the island has been affectionately known as Miyajima, meaning "Shrine Island".

Today, the town has retained its Edo-era look, thanks to the government's strict measures to preserve its local culture. It is famous for the Itsukushima Shrine (after which the island is officially named), with a torii gate that is partially submerged in water. Wild deers wander freely through the streets and parks. Take a walk on the seafront promenade, which is especially attractive when the stone lanterns that line the street are lit in the evening.

To reach the island, take JR ferries or Matsudai ferries, which run up to 10 times per hours, and only take 10 minutes. It's a scenic ride very enjoyable on its own.

What to See

Itsukushima Shrine
The floating torii gate leads the way to the shrine. Depending on the tide, the bright red gate is either "floating" or mired in mud. You can find out the time of the high tide from the tourist information center, but if you are on the island for the whole day, you will see it both ways.

The shrine itself, a World Heritage site, is a red-lacquered complex with halls and pathways on stilts - originally built so that commoners can visit the sacred ground without defiling it with their footprints.

Daisho-in
Hidden in the hills and off of the trodden path, Daisho-in Temple is easily missed. Look for the golden prayer wheels that are said to bring fortune upon anyone who touches them, and the Henjokutsu Cave, an eerie but fascinating collection of Buddhist icons. The temple grounds are a welcome respite from the crowds as well.

Experiences

Mt. Misen Hike
If you are spending the day on the island, hike up Mt. Misen for gorgeous views of the island and the sea. The hike takes about an hour. You can also take the ropeway to an observatory near the top, and hike from there, which will only take 30 minutes.

Miyajima Oyster Festival

Miyajima and its surrounding waters have many flourishing oyster farms that produce oysters famous for their large size, tenderness and juiciness. The Miyajima Oyster Festival is held over two days in early February every year. You'll find fragrant fried oysters, okonomiyaki with oyster fillings, and the famous oyster hot pots flavored with miso, perfect for the winter. There is also a direct sales corner where you'll see locals stopping by for fresh oysters.
Location: In front of Miyajima Pier, Hatsukaichi-shi

Buy
Strangely, Miyajima is famous for rice scoops, the spatula-like wooden spoons used to serve cooked rice. Legend has it that a monk invented it a long time ago, and the wooden device is uniquely able to serve rice without affecting its flavor. You can purchase these along the main shopping street, Omotesando, and look at the World's Largest Spatula showcased here.

Another local treat is deer droppings. No, not as fertilizer - these are crunchy chocolates in the shape of droppings, in the honor of the local deers that roam the island.

Other good souvenirs include miniature floating toriis, and souvenir boxes of sweets. There is also a Hello Kitty Miyajima-themed shop right on Omotesando.

Eat

Oyster and other seafood dominate the menu on Miyajima. Try to steer away from the seafront restaurants, and go for the simpler eateries in the shopping streets near the shrine. There is also refreshment on top of Mt. Misen, with a bit of a price hike.

Momji Manju
These small cakes shaped like maple leaves are traditionally made with sweet bean paste, but cheese, chocolate and other fillings

have become popular. On Omotesando, you can watch some shops make them fresh, and buy packaged ones for family and friends back home. There is also a fried option with a crispy surface, and a soft and sweet center. Be careful though - these are the favorite of local deer as well!

Stay Safe

There is currently a deer feeding ban on Miyajima to control their numbers. As such, the remaining deer popular has become increasingly bold, and will root around bags and backpacks for food - even if the bags are worn on your body! Most deer are relatively tame, but up on Mt. Misen, there are a few who have not had their antlers removed, so take care around them.

There is also a colony of monkeys on the mountain. You might find them hanging around the ropeway station at the peak. Try not to leave food around, or make sudden movements toward them. They likely will not approach you otherwise.

The hike up Mt. Misen is not for everyone, and there are no guide stations along the way. While people of most ages and fitness levels can handle it, take care to consider your own situation.

PART II – CUSTOMIZE YOUR ITINERARY BASED ON YOUR INTERESTS

HISTORICAL AND CULTURAL DESTINATIONS

NARA

Dating back to the 700's, Nara is a capital more ancient than Kyoto. It would be a mistake to skip Nara in lieu of the more popular Kyoto, as it boasts of a collection of cultural and historical sights older than Kyoto's, just as preserved, and most importantly, far less crowded.

See

Nara Park
This sprawling green space contains almost everything you'll want to see in Nara. The legend is that the god of Kasuga Taisha came to Nara riding a white deer, which enjoys protected status as envoys of the god. These cute little animals have gotten used to attention, and now just harass indulgent tourists and annoyed shopkeepers for biscuits.

Nara Deer Park, Nara

Tōdai-ji Temple
Home to Daibutsu, the largest Buddha statue in Japan, Tōdai-ji is a World Heritage Site, and includes the Daibutsu-den, which is said to be the largest wooden building in the world.
Address: 406-1 Zoshicho, Nara 630-8211

Kōfuku-ji
This Temple contains a three-story and a five-story pagoda, which contends with Toji pagoda for the title of the tallest pagoda in Japan.
Address: 48 Noborioji-cho, Nara

Nara National Museum
The national museum contains one of the world's best collections of Buddhist art, including an impressive collection of statues.
Address: 50 Noborioji-cho, Nara

Kasuga-yama Hill Primeval Forest

Enjoy a walk through this wild, undeveloped forest. The path is clearly marked.

NIKKO

Just north of Tokyo, Nikko is home to the mausoleums of the Tokugawa Shoguns. Very unlike most Japanese temples and shrines, these mausoleums are gaudy and ornate, with multi-colored carvings and decorated with gold leaves. The magnificent forest of over 13,000 cedar trees cover the rest of the area, lending some understated refinement to the otherwise ostentatious Nikko.

Nikko / Tanaka Juuyoh

Nikko National Park
Located a few hours from Tokyo, Nikko National Park is the perfect destination for a day trip away from the neon lights. With its natural vista including plateaus, waterfalls, lakes, forests, and rivers, dotted by Nikko's famously ornate shrines, temples, and bridges. There are also plenty of hiking, camping, skiing, and other activities, as well as some great onsen hot spring resorts.

Nikko Toshogu Shrine
Here at Toshogu lies the founder of the Tokugawa dynasty, Tokugawa Ieyasu. This most extravagant tomb, setting the tone

for others to follow, took two years and the efforts of 15,000 workers to complete.

Take a few flights of steps up to the Sacred Stable, housing a white horse. You might recognize the famous symbol here - the carving of the three wise monkeys, who "hear no evil, see no evil, speak no evil".
Address: 2301 Sannai, Nikko, Tochigi Prefecture

Taiyuin-byo Shrine
This smaller, but generally considered artistically superior shrine, belongs to the grandson of Ieyasu, Tokugawa Iemitsu.
Address: 2307 Sannai, Nikko, Tochigi Prefecture

Futarasan Shrine
Rather than emperors, Futarasan is dedicated to the spirits of Nikko's three holy mountains, Mt. Nantai, Mt. Nyoho, and Mt. Taro.
Address: 2307 Sannai, Nikko, Tochigi Prefecture

Kegon Falls
Kegon is one of the highest waterfalls in Japan at 97 meters. The scenery is especially beautiful in the autumn, when leaves change color, but traffic and crowds are also the worst at that time as a result.
Address: 2479-2 Chugushi, Nikko 321-1661, Tochigi Prefecture

Eat

The specialty of Nikko is "yuba", the thin layer that forms on top in the tofu making process. Even if you are not a fan of tofu, yuka tastes pretty good, especially with soba, Japanese buckwheat noodle. In a packaged form, yuba is also a great edible souvenir from the region.

TAKAYAMA

Takayama / Flickr

Takayama is a city near the northern Japan Alps of Gifu prefecture, in the Chubu region of Japan. It is famous for its Edo-style streets, filled with houses sporting the traditional style roof shaped like hands in prayer to protect against snow, known as gassho-zukuri.

What to See

Mida Minzoka Mura Folk Village
Real historical buildings make up this attractive open-air museum, which essentially recreates an entire village. The Walk around, and you can see artisans work in the buildings. You can buy their handmade crafts, or even try to make something yourself.
Address: 1 Chome-590 Kamiokamotomachi, Takayama, Gifu Prefecture

Sanmachi Suji
This pretty section of the old Takayama consists of three narrow lanes, packed with traditional shops in wooden buildings. You'll

find sake breweries and little boutiques, as well as museums housed in some of the larger merchant houses.

Takayama Jinya
Dating from the time of the shogun, this government building now contains displays on the way the local government of Japan worked in the Edo era.
Address: 1-5 Hachikenmachi, Takayama 506-0012, Gifu Prefecture

MIYAJIMA (Itsukushima)

Located off the coast of Hiroshima, the island of Itsukushima offers one of the finest views of Japan. This little island first came on the scene in 806 AD, when the monk Kobo Daishi ascended Mt. Misen and established the mountain as an ascetic site for the Shingon sect of Buddhism. Ever since the island has been affectionately known as Miyajima, meaning "Shrine Island".

Today, the town has retained its Edo-era look, thanks to the government's strict measures to preserve its local culture. It is famous for the Itsukushima Shrine (after which the island is officially named), with a torii gate that is partially submerged in water. Wild deers wander freely through the streets and parks. Take a walk on the seafront promenade, which is especially attractive when the stone lanterns that line the street are lit in the evening.

To reach the island, take JR ferries or Matsudai ferries, which run up to 10 times per hours, and only take 10 minutes. It's a scenic ride very enjoyable on its own.

What to See

Itsukushima Shrine
The floating torii gate leads the way to the shrine. Depending on the tide, the bright red gate is either "floating" or mired in mud. You can find out the time of the high tide from the tourist information center, but if you are on the island for the whole day, you will see it both ways.

The shrine itself, a World Heritage site, is a red-lacquered complex with halls and pathways on stilts - originally built so that commoners can visit the sacred ground without defiling it with their footprints.

Daisho-in

Hidden in the hills and off of the trodden path, Daisho-in Temple is easily missed. Look for the golden prayer wheels that are said to bring fortune upon anyone who touches them, and the Henjokutsu Cave, an eerie but fascinating collection of Buddhist icons. The temple grounds are a welcome respite from the crowds as well.

Experiences

Mt. Misen Hike

If you are spending the day on the island, hike up Mt. Misen for gorgeous views of the island and the sea. The hike takes about an hour. You can also take the ropeway to an observatory near the top, and hike from there, which will only take 30 minutes.

Miyajima Oyster Festival

Miyajima and its surrounding waters have many flourishing oyster farms that produce oysters famous for their large size, tenderness and juiciness. The Miyajima Oyster Festival is held over two days in early February every year. You'll find fragrant fried oysters, okonomiyaki with oyster fillings, and the famous oyster hot pots flavored with miso, perfect for the winter. There is also a direct sales corner where you'll see locals stopping by for fresh oysters.

Location: In front of Miyajima Pier, Hatsukaichi-shi

Buy

Strangely, Miyajima is famous for rice scoops, the spatula-like wooden spoons used to serve cooked rice. Legend has it that a monk invented it a long time ago, and the wooden device is uniquely able to serve rice without affecting its flavor. You can purchase these along the main shopping street, Omotesando, and look at the World's Largest Spatula showcased here.

Another local treat is deer droppings. No, not as fertilizer - these are crunchy chocolates in the shape of droppings, in the honor of the local deers that roam the island.

Other good souvenirs include miniature floating toriis, and souvenir boxes of sweets. There is also a Hello Kitty Miyajima-themed shop right on Omotesando.

Eat

Oyster and other seafood dominate the menu on Miyajima. Try to steer away from the seafront restaurants, and go for the simpler eateries in the shopping streets near the shrine. There is also refreshment on top of Mt. Misen, with a bit of a price hike.

Momji Manju
These small cakes shaped like maple leaves are traditionally made with sweet bean paste, but cheese, chocolate and other fillings have become popular. On Omotesando, you can watch some shops make them fresh, and buy packaged ones for family and friends back home. There is also a fried option with a crispy surface, and a soft and sweet center. Be careful though - these are the favorite of local deer as well!

Stay Safe

There is currently a deer feeding ban on Miyajima to control their numbers. As such, the remaining deer popular has become increasingly bold, and will root around bags and backpacks for food - even if the bags are worn on your body! Most deer are relatively tame, but up on Mt. Misen, there are a few who have not had their antlers removed, so take care around them.

There is also a colony of monkeys on the mountain. You might find them hanging around the ropeway station at the peak. Try not to leave food around, or make sudden movements toward them. They likely will not approach you otherwise.

The hike up Mt. Misen is not for everyone, and there are no guide stations along the way. While people of most ages and fitness levels can handle it, take care to consider your own situation.

BEPPU

Situated along the coast and pressed by mountains, Beppu is a thin and long city famous for its numerous hot springs, and several thermal vents that are too hot for springs, known as its eight "hells".

Beppu / Flickr

What to See

<u>The Hells</u>
They sound terrifying, but the hells of Beppu are actually awesome to behold. These multi-colored volcanic pits of boiling water and mud are too hot to be diluted into viable hot springs, as the temperature can go up to 122 to 210 °F.

Experience

<u>Onsen</u>
Beppu is onsen heaven! The town has several on offer, but the Takegawara Onsen is a Meiji-era classic, and considered the top onsen in the town.

If you have time, try out the whole experience, which starts with you changing into a yukata, a traditional Japanese robe. You then lay down in the sand pit, and an attendant will shovel hot sand on you. Ask them to snap a picture of you buried in sand! After ten minutes, you'll get digged out, and take a shower, before heading to the hot bath.
Address: 16-23   Motomachi,   Beppu,   Oita   Prefecture

NATURE AND OUTDOORS

MT. FUJI

The magnificent Mt. Fuji, at over 12,000 feet, is Japan's highest mountain, and its perfectly symmetrical cone shape one of the most recognizable national symbols of the country. Located about an hour west of Tokyo on the main island of Honshu, Mt. Fuji can be seen from the city on a clear day. Aside from the mountain itself, the area also boasts 25 UNESCO sites of cultural interests, giving you plenty of do and see for a day away from the city.

Mt. Fuji

One Day Itinerary

When to Visit: The official climbing season lasts for only two months, from July to August. Even during these months, when Tokyo often swelters in 40°C heat, temperatures at the top can be below freezing at night and climbers must dress adequately.

Climbing outside the official season is extremely dangerous without alpine climbing experience and equipment.

Getting There: Mt. Fuji can be approached from all sides, but note that transport schedules are sharply cut outside the official climbing season in July and August.

The easiest option for reaching the slopes of Mt. Fuji from Tokyo is to take the Keio express bus from Shinjuku in Tokyo. The direct bus takes 2 to 2.5 hours, depending on traffic, costs ¥2600, and takes you directly to the start of the climb at Kawaguchiko 5th Station. To buy a ticket, take the west exit at Shinjuku station, then follow the circle of bus stops to the left. The Keio building is on the corner near stop 26, right across from Yodobashi Camera. You can reserve a seat for free at Keio express bus. You will still need to pay for your ticket at the station (cash only).

The most economical approach is by Odakyu train from Shinjuku to Gotemba, although you will have to change trains and the price difference is rather minimal.

The Climb: Consider starting out in late morning, and see the majestic sunset from the summit. Most people take 4 to 8 hours at walking speed to get to the top, and another 2 to 4 hours to descend.

The most popular starting point is Kawaguchiko 5th Station, which begins with an initial stretch of flowery meadows. The bulk of the hike is through jagged volcanic landscape, however, and becomes steeper as you progress.

There are also climbing tours offered by numerous travel companies throughout Japan. These tours may include round trip bus fare, climbing guide, hut, dinner, breakfast (packed rice box), and a visit to a hot spring after the descent. Prices tend to be expensive though: a one-day "superman" tour costs around

¥20000 and a more leisurely two-day approach (including overnight stay) is over ¥30000. Most of these tours are conducted in Japanese and stick firmly to the trodden path.

Getting Around: Once on the mountain the only way of getting around is on foot. The sole exception is horseback riding, available on the Fujiguchiko trail between the 5th and 7th stations only for the steep price of ¥14,000.

Five Lakes
The most popular places for sightseeing tours of Fuji and surroundings are <u>Hakone</u>, to the east of Mt. Fuji towards Tokyo, and the <u>Fuji Five Lakes</u>, located just north of the mountain. Note, however, that Fuji is notoriously shy and is wreathed in clouds most of the time: it's entirely possible to drive around the mountain and never see it. Visibility tends to be the worst in the hot, muggy summer and the best in the winter, when the air is dry and clear.

Murayama Senjen Jinja (Temple)
Before the tourists go to the 5th level of the Mt Fuji, they must visit the Murayama Sengen Jinja temple because Japanese people believe that Mt Fuji is a sacred mountain firmly connected to God.

ISHIKAGI ISLAND

Many visitors stop by the second-largest but most populated of the islands in Okinawa, for great beaches and water sports on the island's northern coast.

Kabira Bay
A stunning bay at the northwestern corner of Ishikagi, Kabira has emerald blue water with perfect yellow-white sand. You can walk along the coast, but the fast-moving tides make swimming impossible. You can take a glass-bottom boat tour to get a view of the transparent shallow sea, or take a landside view from Kabira Park, a promenade complete with viewing pavilion that stretches along the coast, above the beach itself.

Yonehara Beach
Yonehara is known for nice sand and even better coral reefs. It is particularly popular with snorkelers, as the reef begins within meters of the beach. At times, the rip currents can be notoriously

strong, however, so heed the signs that describe which areas should be avoided.

Experiences

Scuba diving, kayaking, snorkeling and other water sports are all popular activities in Ishikagi's beautiful waters full of coral reefs. There are a large number of dive operators, but rates are mostly standardized at around ¥12,000 for two boat dives (not including gear rental).

If you want to see something special, head to Manta Scramble, just off Ishikagi's north coast, a legendary manta ray spotting place where large groups of manta rays are almost guaranteed during autumn.

SAPPORO

The capital and the largest city of the Island of Hokkaido, Sapporo is a relatively young city, with occupation only since the mid-1800's. As such, it has little in the way of traditional architecture, but makes up for it in lovely tree-filled boulevards in the summer, and lots of facilities for snow sports during the winter.

What to See

Mt. Moiwa
From Mt. Moiwa, you get a good view of not only Sapporo, but also the Sea of Japan. The view at night is especially beautiful. You can either hike up the trails, or take the cable car to the middle of the mountain, then a mini cable car to the top.

Odori Park
Sapporo's most famous park, Odori is situated in the center of the town, and is considered a symbol of the city. The narrow and stretched out strip of land is filled with flowers, trees, and fountains during the summer. It is a welcoming sanctuary from the bustling city.

Sapporo Beer Museum
This little museum, sun by the Sapporo Brewing Company, offers free guided tours on the history of beer making in Japan, and the process of brewing. At the end of the tour, you get to taste their different beers, and get a few more pints at the beer garden next door.

Experience

Sapporo Snow Festival

Sapporo Snow Festival
If in town in early February, you simply cannot miss the Sapporo Snow Festival, the city's largest event. Think of the festival of an amusement park made of ice! There is an ice sculpture competition attracting artists from around the world.

HAKODATE

The largest city in southern Hokkaido, Hakodate is one of the oldest trading cities in Japan, and as a result, shows signs of foreign influences in everything, from its custom to its architecture.

Hakodate / Kurosawa Michiyo

What to See

Mt. Hakodate
In clear weather, Mt. Hakodate offers one of the three best night views in all of Japan - or of the world, if you ask the locals.

Goryōkaku Tower
The 90-meter viewing platform in the star-shaped fort offers a striking view in any season - in the spring, you can see 1,600 sakura trees all in blossom. In the summer, you are treated to lots of greenery, while in the autumn, you can see the changing foliage. In the winter, the entire fort is covered in snow and

illuminated at night. There are displays that tell the story of the fort itself, including an English pamphlet.
Address: 44 Goryōkakuchō, Hakodate, Hokkaido Prefecture

Eat (Hokkaido in General)

Fresh Seafood
Being an island, Hokkaido is known for lots of fresh seafood. Their hairy crabs and king crabs are especially good. And of course, fresh sushi!

Hakodate in particular is known for squid, cooked in a version of ramen, with squid stock instead of the usual pork.

Drink Hokkaido Milk Products
Inland Hokkaido is known for its dairy products, for its cows are very well cared for, eating only clean grass from rich and fertile soil. No chemical feed for these little grazers! Anything from fresh milk, yogurt, to ice cream is great here. Even if you don't normally like milk, give it a try and you might be very surprised.

Sapporo Beer
Sapporo is of course home to the most famous Japanese beer brand, the Sapporo beer. Try it anywhere in Hokkaido, and you won't be disappointed.

NOZAWA ONSEN (NAGANO)

This traditional village, in the Nagano prefecture, has been a hidden gem until recently. While it boasts of 13 public onsens that offer the usual health benefits and a number of private ones within the ryokans and hotels, it is alpine skiing that has made the place renowned in recent years.

With its cobble stoned streets and houses, Nozawa has a quaint rural charm. During ski season, many restaurants pop up, some in local homes. On January 15th of each year, one of the three major fire festivals is held here. The central ceremony involves a large wooden shrine with 42 year olds sitting on the top, while 25 year olds (both ages are considered unlucky) below attempt to engage in battle, and light the shrine on fire. There are also fireworks, sake, and lots of fire.

OFF THE BEATEN PATH DESTINATIONS

NAGOYA

Nagoya is the Detroit of Japan. Home to automaking giants Toyota, Honda, and Mitsubishi, it is the fourth largest city and one of the country's major economic centers.

What to See

Toyota Commemorative Museum of Industry and Technology
Did you know that Toyota used to be an industrial loom manufacturer? You can find out all about the auto giant's history at this museum built on the site of one of its original loom factories. There are displays from the company's history, from loom machinery to car display halls, and a hands-on "Technoland" with interactive science exhibits that adults and kids will both love. Brochures and guides are available in English and a few other languages.
Address: 4-1-35 Noritakeshinmachi, Nishi-ku, Nagoya 451-0051, Aichi Prefecture

Nagoya Castle
This famous landmark, with the two renowned golden carps on the roof, belonged to Oda Nobunaga, a Japanese warlord. Like many other historical sights across Japan, Nagoya Castle was destroyed in the war, and rebuilt in concrete. There is an interesting museum, an observation deck, and gardens on its ground.
Address: 1-1 Honmaru, Naka Ward, Nagoya, Aichi Prefecture

Atsuta Jingu (Atsuta Shrine)
Atsuta Jingu is home to the sacred Kusanagi no mitsurugi sword, one of the three imperial regalia of Japan. Unfortunately, only the emperor and a few high priests are allowed to view it in person.

But there are over 4,000 other artifacts you are allowed to see, and the shrine hosts 70 festivals every year.
Address: 1-1-1 Jingu, Atsuta-ku, Nagoya 456-0031,Aichi Prefecture

Atsuta Jingu, Nagoya / Flickr

Experiences

Osu Shopping Arcade
This is no ordinary Japanese shopping mall. Osu is a series of old-style shopping arcades - mom-and-pop stores, ¥100 shops, traditional crafts, used computers and a fantastic range of clothing stores. Off of the main street, which extends from Osu Kannan temple in the west to Bansho-ji Temple and Otsu-dori street in the east, there are also many different specialty shops on side streets.
Address: Osu Naka-ku, Nagoya 460-0011, Aichi Prefecture

Eat

Miso

Miso is Nagoya's local specialty. This sauce made from fermented soybeans and grains is widely used in broth across Japanese cuisine. Try misokatsu, fried pork cutlet with a rich miso-based sauce.

Shrimp Tempura

Shrimp tempura is also particularly good in Nagoya - try it wrapped in rice and dried seaweed, a little bit like a big sushi, in a portable package known as a tenmusu.

KOBE

Expats love Kobe, a great cosmopolitan port city with an international flavor. Modern, but not over the top, it is consistently ranked No.1 as the best place to live in Japan, and an often missed jewel by tourists.

Kobe

What to See

Ijinkan
Kobe has a unique architectural style, specifically with a host of older western-style houses, some dating back to the 1800's, when Japan first opened up for foreign trade. The Ijinkan, or foreign houses, are clustered in the Kitano area. Many of these houses were renovated and now operate as cafes or museums.

Mt. Rokko
Mt. Rokko is a favorite hiking destination for residents of Kobe as well as Osaka. It offers a glittering view of Osaka Bay, and hosts the Mt. Rokko Ice Festival every February. Note that outside July and August, the cable car routes close before sunset during the rest of the year.

Experiences

Arima Onsen

One of Japan's oldest hot spring onsen resorts, Arima is still consistently ranked as the top onsen in western Japan. The resort offers two types of hot spring waters - the Kinsen, or "gold water", which is brown with iron deposits and good for skin ailments and muscle pains, and Ginsen, or "silver water", which contains radium and carbonate, said is said to cure various muscle and joint ailments. The town has two public bath houses, and many ryokans with their private springs.

Eat

Kobe beef is of course a must-try in the city it is named after. It is a very expensive beef that is famously marbled, fatty and tender. You'll have to splurge - expect to pay around ¥10,000 per head.

After the splurge, save some money and have some sobameshi, a cheap and delicious Kobe favorite concocted of fried rice and noodles mixed together.

Drink

Sake

Kobe is a well-known center of sake production, famous for its fine mountain water used in brewing. There are many breweries and museums open to the public.

Sake Containers

FUKUOKA

Fukuoka is a modern city - most of its current buildings are new. Historically, the central river divided the city into two parts, Hakata, and Fukuoka, before their merge in 1889. Many landmarks, like the main railway station and port, are still known as Hakata, after the city they were situated in.

What to See

Ohori Park and Maizuru Park
With its 2km jogging track and pleasant ground, Ohori Park in city center is popular with locals throughout the year, and organizes events like fireworks every summer. Next door in Maizuru Park, you can see the ruins of Fukuoka Castle and a good view of the city.
Address: 1-2 Ohorikoen, Chuo-ku, Fukuoka 810-0051,Fukuoka Prefecture

Gion Area
This section of the city is home to several historical shrines and Buddhist temples, including Kushida Shrine from the 8th century, Tocho-ji Temple with its 10.8 meter tall wooden Great Buddha, and Shofuku-ji, Japan's first Zen temple.

Nokonoshima Island
If time permits, hop to the small Nokonoshima Island in Hakata Bay for hiking, swimming, camping and other activities in nature. It's only a 10 minute ferry ride from Fukuoka.

Experience

Watch Sumo Wrestling
In November, you can attend sumo matches in Fukuoka. You might occasionally run into sumo wrestlers on the streets too.

Eat

Hakata Ramen

Fukuoka has its own style of ramen - Hakata Ramen, known for a pungent smell thanks to a pork rib broth called tonkotsu. It's delicious, and if you save the broth, you can order a refill of noodles for around ¥300 at many places.

NAOSHIMA ISLAND

The entire island of Naoshima, in the Seto Inland Sea of Japan, is renowned for its large collection of contemporary art galleries. As part of the "Art House Project", many houses on the island, originally settled as a coastal town back in the 1400's, have been radically transformed into galleries. After getting your fill of contemporary art, head to the beach for a swim, or to the mountains for a hike. You'll easily pass a whole day here!

Benesse House Complex

The first, and still one of the best contemporary art museums on the island, Benesse House displays the works of Andy Warhol, Richard Long, Bruce Nauman, and many others. The building itself is a piece of art designed by world famous Japanese architect Tadao Ando. You'll also find several outdoor exhibits surrounding the house.

Chichu Art Museum

Also designed by Tadao Ando, Chichu Art Museum was completed in 2006 to extensive media attention in Japan. At this museum, you'll find the works of Claude Monet, Walter de Maria, and James Turrell. It is the most popular attraction on the island, so you'll want to head there early to avoid the crowd. On Fridays and Saturdays, the museum hosts a night program for Turrell's work, "Open Sky", at sunset.

OKUNOSHIMA (RABBIT ISLAND)

During the war, this small island in the Inland Sea of Japan was the site of a top secret poison gas factory. Thankfully today, it is known for something far less nefarious - rabbits. Apparently after the war, rabbits were set in the island and they began to breed as rabbits do. Before the settlers know it, the island is swarming with cuddly bunnies.

The rabbits on the island are very tame. Visitors should bring food for them, or purchase carrots, cabbage, and rabbit feed at the hotel. To protect the bunnies, dogs and cats are forbidden from entering.

AOSHIMA (CAT ISLAND)

Feral cats rule supreme on Aoshima, where they were first introduced to deal with a mice problem. After multiplying for many years, these little fur balls outnumber humans six to one - more than 120 cats live on this island in southern Japan, with only a handful of human, mostly pensioners left behind by waves of migrants seeking work in the cities.

Note that this isn't really a tourist attraction. The island has no restaurants, cars, shops, or kiosks. But that hasn't stopped cat lovers from dropping by and making a few new friends.

88 TEMPLE PILGRIMAGE CIRCUIT IN SHIKOKU

Japan's most famous pilgrimage route, this circuit of 1,200 km loops around the island of Shikoku, and contains the 88 temples associated with the renowned monk Kukai. Traditional pilgrims complete the journey on foot - which would take 30 to 60 days, but nowadays, many travelers use cars, taxis, buses, bicycles, or motorcycles.

PLANNING YOUR TRIP

EXCHANGE RATES

Unit = Yen (¥)

Rates are calculated at the time of this writing. Please check before your departure for the up-to-date exchange rate.

USD: 1 Dollar = 123 Yen
Canadian Dollar: 1 Dollar = 100 Yen
British Pounds: 1 Pound = 192 Yen
Euro: 1 Euro = 138 Yen
Australian Dollar: 1 Dollar = 95 Yen

VISA INFORMATION

Generally, no visa required for visitors (who do not plan to engage in business in Japan). They can obtain landing permission on arrival without a visa. This is usually valid for a stay of up to 90 days. For more information on visas to Japan, visit: Japanese Ministry of Foreign Affairs website- http://www.mofa.go.jp/j_info/visit/visa/

US: eligible for visa-free stay, up to 90 days
Canada: eligible for visa-free stay, up to 90 days
Australia: eligible for visa-free stay, up to 90 days
United Kingdom: eligible for visa-free stay, up to 180 days
Germany: eligible for visa-free stay, up to 180 days
France: eligible for visa-free stay, up to 90 days

Japanese Holidays/Festivals

New Year is the most important holiday in Japan. The country is essentially shut down between December 30 and January 3.

Hanami, or cherry blossom viewing, takes place in March and April. Japanese organize outdoor picnics en masse, and drink quite a bit. The flowers blossom at slightly different times every year depending on the weather, but Japanese TV, and their audience, track their progress obsessively.

Golden Week, the longest holiday lasting from April 27 to May 6, when there are four public holidays within the week. Everyone goes on extended vacation, plane tickets and hotel prices soar as a result to multiples of normal prices. Try to take your vacation before or after Golden Week, to avoid paying extra.

<u>Major Japanese Holidays</u>

January 1 - **New Year's Day** (ganjitsu or gantan)

January 9 (Second Monday of month) - **Coming-of-Age Day** (seijin no hi)

February 11 - **National Foundation Day** (kenkoku kinen no hi)

March 20 - **Spring Equinox Day** (shunbun no hi)

April 29 - **Showa Day** (showa no hi) - first holiday of Golden Week

May 3 - **Constitution Day** (kenpō kinnenbi)

May 4 - **Greenery Day** (midori no hi)

May 5 - **Children's Day** (kodomo no hi) - last holiday of Golden Week

July 16 (third Monday of month) - **Marine Day** (umi no hi)

September 17 (third Monday of month) - **Respect-for-the-Aged Day** (keirō no hi)

September 22 - **Autumnal Equinox Day** (shuubun no hi)

November 3 - **Culture Day** (bunka no hi)

November 23 - **Labor Thanksgiving Day** (kinrō kansha no hi)

December 23 - **The Emperor's Birthday** (tennō tanjōbi)

Carrying Your Passport with You

Once in Japan, you must carry your passport (or Alien Registration Card or Residence Card, if applicable) with you at all times. If caught in a random check without it (and nightclub raids are not uncommon), you'll be detained until somebody can fetch it for you. Don't panic - first offenders who apologize are usually let off with a warning

ESSENTIAL JAPANESE CULTURE TO KNOW

Tipping

Tips are not expected in Japan, even though the country's service is legendary. Attempting to tip from a westerner can even be seen as an insult, and the wait staff is likely to run after you to return the money you "forgot". Unless you are in a high-end ryokan or with an English-speaking tour guide, you are safer not to tip.

Manners and Showing Respect

As with many East Asian cultures, a person's family name comes before their given name in Japan. In addition, using only someone's given name when speaking to or about them is very personal, and should only be used between close friends. At all other times, use family name plus -san, a suffix approximately like "Mr." or "Ms."

Japanese people bow to greet each other, even when they are on the phone! As a foreigner, try to at least bob your head to greet your Japanese associates. Sometimes, in order to be accommodating, Japanese will offer a handshake to a westerner.

Be on time! There is no such thing as "fashionably late" in Japan. You will only be considered rude.

There is no strict dress code when visiting temples and shrines, but you will feel out of place in shorts or other revealing clothes. Jeans and casual clothing are fine, but remember to remove your shoes when entering temples. There are usually slippers for you to change into.

Japan has an avid drinking culture. Never refuse a drink - it's considered very rude - but accept it and sip at your drink. Make sure your glass is half full.

USEFUL JAPANESE TERMS AND PHRASES

You'll likely be able to find someone who speaks English and is willing to help you in Japan, famous for their hospitality, but it's always good to have a few key phrases at your command, and to show your politeness and respect with new friends you might make. Remember, to be safe, address everyone by their last name, with -san attached.

Thank you: Arigatoo gozaimasu.

Thank you very much: Doomo arigatoo gozaimasu.

You're welcome: Doo itashimashite.

Please: onegai shimasu

Yes: hai

No: iie

Excuse me: Sumimasen.

Pardon me: Sumimasen.

I'm sorry: Gomen'nasai.

I don't understand: Wakarimasen.

I don't speak Japanese: Nihongo ga wakarimasen.

I don't speak Japanese very well: Nihongo wa amari joozu ja arimasen.

Do you speak English: Eigo o hanashimasu ka?

Speak slowly, please: Yukkuri hanashite kudasai.

Repeat, please: Moo ichido onegai shimasu.

What's your name: Onamae wa nandesu ka?

How are you: Ogenki desu ka?

Do you speak English: Eigo o hanashimasu ka?

Where is the subway: Chikatetsu wa doko desu ka?

Is the tip included: Chippu wa fukumarete imasu ka?

How much does that cost: Kore wa ikura desu ka?

Is there a public phone here: Koko ni kooshuudenwa ga arimasu ka?

Can I get on the internet: Intaanetto o tsukattemo iidesu ka?

Can you help me: Tetsudatte itadakemasu ka?

Where is the bathroom: Ofuro wa doko desu ka?

-dori: Street/Avenue

CONCLUSION

We hope this pocket guide helps you navigate Japan and find the most memorable and authentic things to do, see, and eat. While it is difficult to experience everything on a short vacation in Japan, that does not mean you will not have an amazing time during your stay. We are excited for the unforgettable memories you will create on your trip!

Thank you for purchasing our pocket guide. After you've read this guide, we'd really appreciate your honest book review!

Sincerely,
The Wanderlust Pocket Guides Team

Also by Wanderlust Pocket Guides:

BEST OF TOKYO: YOUR #1 ITINERARY PLANNER FOR WHAT TO SEE, DO, AND EAT

BEST OF KYOTO: YOUR #1 ITINERARY PLANNER FOR WHAT TO SEE, DO, AND EAT

BEST OF TOKYO AND KYOTO BOOK SET

Available on Amazon.com

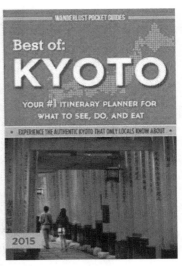

CREDITS

Original map vectors: Wikipedia Archives

COPYRIGHT AND DISCLAIMER

Made in the USA
San Bernardino, CA
13 August 2015